C++ Strategies and Tactics

Addison-Wesley Professional Computing Series

Brian W. Kernighan, Consulting Editor

Ken Arnold/John Peyton, *A C User's Guide to ANSI C*

Tom Cargill, *C++ Programming Style*

David A. Curry, *UNIX® System Security: A Guide for Users and System Administrators*

Scott Meyers, *Effective C++: 50 Specific Ways to Improve Your Programs and Designs*

Robert B. Murray, *C++ Strategies and Tactics*

Craig Partridge, *Gigabit Networking*

Radia Perlman, *Interconnections: Bridges and Routers*

David M. Piscitello/A. Lyman Chapin, *Open Systems Networking: TCP/IP and OSI*

Stephen A. Rago, *UNIX® System V Network Programming*

W. Richard Stevens, *Advanced Programming in the UNIX® Environment*

W. Richard Stevens, *TCP/IP Illustrated, Volume 1: The Protocols*

C++ Strategies and Tactics

Robert B. Murray

ADDISON-WESLEY PUBLISHING COMPANY

Reading, Massachusetts   Menlo Park, California   New York   Don Mills, Ontario
Wokingham, England   Amsterdam   Bonn   Sydney   Singapore   Tokyo   Madrid   San Juan
Paris   Seoul   Milan   Mexico City   Taipei

The publisher offers discounts on this book when ordered in quantity for special sales. For more information please contact:

Corporate & Professional Publishing Group
Addison-Wesley Publishing Company
One Jacob Way
Reading, Massachusetts 01867

Library of Congress Cataloging-in-Publication Data

Murray, Robert B.
    C++ strategies and tactics / Robert B. Murray.
        p. cm. — (Addison-Wesley professional computing series)
    Includes index.
    ISBN 0-201-56382-7 (pbk.)
    1. C++ (Computer program language) I. Title. II. Series.
QA76.73.C15M87 1993
005.13'3—dc20   92-45287
                                                      CIP

AT&T

ISBN 0-201-56382-7
Text printed on recycled and acid-free paper.
3 4 5 6 7 8 9 10- CRW -96959493
Third Printing: September 1993

For Lorraine
and Sarah Beth

Contents

Reviews

Preface

In the hands of an expert, C++ helps designers and programmers build systems that are modular, maintainable, and fast. To the novice, however, the size of the language can be intimidating. There are a lot of features in C++ and it takes some experience to learn which ones are appropriate for any situation.

This book is intended to enhance and expedite that learning process. Most successful C++ programmers cannot recite chapter and verse from the language rules; instead, they have acquired a set of idioms and techniques that have worked well for them. Our goal is to help the C++ novice learn those idioms that have been most useful in practice. We also point out some of the most common pitfalls.

We do not try to cover the entire language and we leave the ultra-precise definitions of language semantics to the reference manuals. Instead, we concentrate on helping the reader build programs that can be understood by someone who is *not* a C++ language lawyer. We not only discuss techniques for making programs elegant and fast; we also show how to make them easier to understand and maintain.

Acknowledgments

Almost none of the ideas and programming idioms in this book are my invention. My goal has been to present, in a way that allows novice C++ programmers to learn them quickly, what I consider to be the most important strategies and tactics I have learned from others in the eight years I have been using C++. Some of these lessons were learned by studying actual development projects as they moved from C to C++; others came from discussions with talented individuals.

Many of the best ideas on templates and library design, including the ideas behind many of the container classes in this book, came from classes in the USL Standard Components that were originally designed by Martin Carroll, Andrew Koenig, and Jonathan Shopiro. I claim exclusive ownership of any errors in my versions. Andrew Koenig was a valuable resource as the local C++ language lawyer. The participants in the "C++ Strategies and Tactics" seminars I presented at several conferences helped inspire this book and refine its ideas. Other important ideas came from Tom Cargill, John Carolan, Jim Coplien, Mark Linton, Gerald Schwarz, and of course Bjarne Stroustrup, who also invented the C++ programming language that made the book possible in the first place.

Brian Kernighan read several drafts of this book, and his excellent feedback has been a lot of help. I would also like to thank David Annatone, Steve Buroff, Tom Cargill, Bill Hopkins, Cay Horstman, Lorraine Juhl, Peter Juhl, Stan Lippman, Dennis Mancl, Scott Meyers, Barbara Moo, Lorraine Weisbrot Murray, Bjarne Stroustrup, Clovis Tondo, Steve Vinoski, and Christopher Van Wyk for their comments on early drafts of this book. Lorraine Weisbrot Murray also contributed the encouragement, understanding, support, and love that helped make the entire effort feasible.

Chapter 0

Introduction

C++ is a big language. A programmer who only knows the rules of C++ is like a chess player who only knows how the pieces move. To succeed, the student must also acquire a set of principles and strategies.

This book is aimed at the novice to intermediate C++ programmer who wants to learn more about using the language, but lacks the time to take a semester length college course. We assume that the reader understands the basics of C++ — what a member function is, the use of `public`, `private`, and `protected`, and so forth. Readers are not expected to be C++ experts; when we discuss the more advanced topics in the language (like multiple inheritance), we include a "Review" in a sidebar that briefly summarizes the rules. We concentrate on the strategies that experience has shown are most effective in practice. We are short on theory and long on examples and practical advice.

We will not stray far off the beaten track. None of the ideas and techniques in this book are ground breaking in any fundamental way, and most of them have been in use by experienced C++ programmers for years. The newest and most innovative ideas are, by their nature, also the riskiest. We hope to steer the novice C++ user *away* from such ideas. With the exception of Chapter 10 ("Exceptions"), which covers a feature that is new to C++, the techniques in this book are all "tried and truc."

We are also not interested in turning the reader into a C++ language lawyer. C++ contains some dark and dusty corners; instead of poking around in the corners, we will point them out and then avoid them. It is not a good idea to write programs that depend on obscure or subtle language rules; even if the author gets it right, the next person who has to maintain the code may not. It is better to stick to the parts of the language that are widely used and understood.

0.1 A note about the code examples

Each of the examples in this book has either been compiled as is, or is excerpted from a larger file that has been compiled. To keep the examples as short as possible, we routinely omit surrounding baggage (such as `#include` directives).

Much of this book deals with interfaces, not implementations. Many of the code examples will therefore omit private parts for clarity:

```
class Something {
    // Private stuff omitted ...
public:
    Something();
};
```

0.2 A road map

Chapter 1 ("Abstraction") discusses the process of choosing the right high level abstractions for a design, with an emphasis on maintaining the distinction between those abstractions and their implementations.

The next two chapters look at the process of turning a a high level abstraction into one or more C++ classes. Chapter 2 ("Classes") covers issues ranging from high level design strategies to low level interface and implementation details. In Chapter 3 ("Handles"), we explore several ways handles are used in class implementations.

The next three chapters introduce the concept of inheritance. Chapter 4 ("Inheritance") discusses the differences between public, protected, and private inheritance, and gives guidelines for the use of each kind of inheritance. Chapter 5 ("Multiple Inheritance") covers the use of more than one base class; we discuss the circumstances under which it should be used, and cover some of MI's thorny details. In Chapter 6 ("Designing for Inheritance") we talk about how to build your classes so that someone else can use them as base classes.

The new templates feature is very powerful and will profoundly affect the way people write C++ programs. We cover templates in detail in Chapters 7

("Templates") and 8 ("Advanced Templates"). Since many C++ users have little experience with templates, we start with the basics, cover some techniques for building effective templates, and then build a variety of templates. These will include templates that implement smart pointers, some simple containers, and finally a more substantial container (a `List` template). We then discuss some of the ways our `List` template could be restructured to make it faster, smaller, and more functional.

Chapter 9 ("Reusability") discusses making a piece of working code into a reusable library: it takes a lot of effort to make reuse more than just a buzzword. We show how the features introduced in the earlier chapters can be used to enhance the robustness, ease of use, and performance of your code.

The new exceptions feature makes it possible to write code without constantly checking for error conditions, but it is also prone to misuse. We talk about how to use it, and how *not* to use it, in Chapter 10 ("Exceptions"). The industry is still learning how to use exceptions, so this chapter is somewhat speculative.

Moving a project from C to C++ involves more than just a change of compilers: projects must get used to a new way of developing software. Chapter 11 will say a few words about the most common technical and human issues encountered by projects adopting C++.

0.3   Questions

Each chapter except this one ends with "In short," which will present, as a bullet list, the key ideas introduced in that chapter, followed by "Questions." The questions are intended to stimulate thought and discussion about both technical issues and human issues: keeping things easy to understand and easy to maintain. Some of these questions have "right" answers; many do not, but we hoped that the discussions they start will be useful.

0.4   The language rules

The current "official" definition of the C++ language is the *Annotated C++ Reference Manual*, by Ellis and Stroustrup[1], often referred to as the "ARM."

---

[1]Ellis, M., and Stroustrup, B., *The Annotated C++ Reference Manual* (Reading, Mass.: Addison–Wesley, 1990).

The ARM is the base document for the ISO/ANSI C++ Standards Committee, an international group of volunteers from industry and academia who are developing a definition for the C++ language that will be both the ANSI and ISO official standard. Statements in this book about the "language rules" are based on the ARM, unless the ISO/ANSI committee has come to a clear consensus on some different behavior. Most of the differences to date have been minor. All C++ users are encouraged to follow the standardization effort.

Chapter 1

Abstraction

Data abstraction is one of the central concepts in object-oriented design. Data abstraction predates object-oriented design; however, the rising popularity of languages like C++ that directly support it has made its use much more widespread.

An *abstract data type* is a user defined type that has two clearly separated parts:

a *public interface* that specifies how users manipulate objects of that type, and

a *private implementation* that is used internally by the type to implement the behavior specified by the public interface.

In C++, the `private` and `public` keywords are used to indicate which parts of a class declaration are implementation and which are interface. In this way, the compiler can ensure that users of a class do not bypass the interface by directly accessing private members. The fact that a class has private members, however, does not mean that it is well designed.

There is another idea that is far more important than the low level language rules for `public` and `private`. This idea is never explicitly checked by the C++ compiler, but is crucial to the design of modular, maintainable programs. This is the concept that every solution to a programming problem has two parts: an *abstract model* that is a mental model of the problem and its solution that the programmer and the user(s) agree on; and the *implementation* that is the particular way the programmer makes a computer reflect the abstraction. In this chapter, we will examine the process of designing, refining, and documenting the abstraction provided by a class. As we shall see, simply writing a manual page and then making the code agree with it is not enough.

There are several reasons why a well thought out and documented abstract model is important:

It's what someone else needs to understand to use your class.
If you are attempting to use a linked-list class, your main concern (at first) should not be the names of the header files, or the names and argument types of the member functions. Rather, you should ask fundamental questions about the abstract model of this class: What operations are supported? Can you move through the list backwards? Can you find the head or tail of the list in constant time? Can the same object be on more than one list? Does the list contain the objects or just references to them? If it contains references, who is responsible for creating and destroying the objects? What happens when an object that is on a list is destroyed? And so forth.

The answers to these questions will have a major impact on the design of any application that uses the linked-list class. (For instance, if your application needs to move both ways through a list, a singly linked list is probably not suitable.)

If you do not understand, *and document*, the abstract model that your class supports, users may decide not to use it (or worse, decide to use it and discover down the road that it was a mistake).

The abstract model is your contract with your users. Since the abstract model can have a strong influence on the design of users' programs, you may find it difficult (if not impossible) to make changes to it that are not upwardly compatible. A decision to remove the capability to back up in a list, for example, would be a disaster for any publicly available `List` class. Why? Some of the users of that class will have designed their entire application around the `List` class abstraction that included being able to back up. That incompatible change in the abstraction is guaranteed to blow some existing users out of the water. If a class is widely used, every feature will become absolutely required for at least one user, and this user will raise a ruckus if you attempt to remove it.

This means that it is especially important to refine and perfect the abstract model before you deliver your library to your customers. A mistake in the implementation can often be fixed in the next release; a mistake in the abstract model (except an error of omission) can persist for the lifetime of the class.

The process of documenting the abstract model often points out important flaws in the design. Early in the design of a software project, we often overestimate our understanding of the problem and our proposed solution. Putting our fuzzy thoughts into clear, precise words helps focus our attention on the parts that have not been thought through. It makes it harder to sweep things under the rug.

Clear documentation of the abstract model makes it possible for others to create new versions of your classes, either by derivation or simple reimplementation. To implement a new version of a class that will work with existing code, you need to match the original code in more than the names and type signatures of the member functions. The new version must conform to the abstract model of the old version.

Understanding the abstract model avoids having the implementation drive the design. Many software designers, whether they realize it or not, have an "obvious" implementation in mind when they design a new class interface. This can have the effect of molding the abstraction to fit the implementation. Not only might this direct the designer to an interface that is not the most natural for the user to understand; it may also let implementation details creep through into the interface, making it hard to change the implementation later.

Of course, the other extreme (doing an interface with complete ignorance of the likely implementation) can also lead to trouble. An interface that is impossible to implement or imposes an unacceptable performance overhead will not help the user no matter how elegant it is. Balancing these concerns is one of the most challenging parts of class design. This last point notwithstanding, designing the abstraction should be a separate activity from designing the implementation. This does not necessarily imply that different people should design the two parts; the point is that the developer should always know whether, at this minute, he or she is working on the abstraction or the implementation.

Thinking only of the abstraction (*not* of the implementation) takes some practice. Deciding what should be, or should not be, in the abstraction, is one of the key skills of the object-oriented designer. We will start to build a small abstraction in the next section.

1.1   A telephone number abstraction

In this section, we will take a first cut at the abstraction for a class that represents a telephone number. We would like this class to represent telephone numbers in a variety of telephony applications (switching systems, billing systems, and so forth).

What is the first step? A good way to begin is to *write a sentence that describes what the object does* (as opposed to what it *is*). The description should be as high level as possible and should say little if anything about the internal structure of the object. This "executive summary" should be so simple that even an executive could understand it.

For example, here is a *bad* executive summary of a telephone number:

> "A telephone number is a three digit area code, followed by a three digit exchange, followed by four digits."

This description says nothing about what a telephone number does or what it interacts with. Instead, it simply makes a statement of the structure of a telephone number. This is not only incomplete in terms of what a telephone number does; it also over-constrains a telephone number. For example, a telephone number that is being dialed by a modem might contain nondigit characters (such as & to tell the modem to wait for a secondary dial tone, or the # and * special keys). More seriously, it constrains the set of telephone numbers to those that are legal for calls between two area codes in the US and Canada.

Here is a better try:

> "A telephone number identifies a particular telephone in the world."

This statement says nothing about how a telephone number is structured; it says something about how another abstraction might use a telephone number.

After you make such a statement, take some time to pick at it. Examine every word with the care that a lawyer would use to examine a legally binding contract. What are the loopholes in this statement? What are the implicit assumptions?

Let's start with the word *identifies*. What does this mean? Does a telephone number uniquely identify a telephone, or can two or more telephones be associated with a single telephone number? In fact, many businesses have banks of telephones that respond to a single telephone number: a local switch will route each incoming call to a phone that is not in use. Also, a telephone number is not a unique identifier for a particular telephone. When you dial "555-1234", the telephone you get depends on the location you are dialing from.

So, a telephone number need not refer to a unique phone, and its meaning depends on where it is used. To reflect this, our next try at an executive summary might be:

> "A telephone number is a key that, when combined with an originating telephone, yields a destination telephone."

This statement includes the dependency on the originating telephone, and drops the implication that the destination telephone is unique. But let's look more closely at the last part of the sentence. Is it right to say that making a phone call gets you the destination telephone? Perhaps, but it may be more accurate to say that making a phone call gets you a *connection* to the destination telephone. What is the difference? It depends on whether the user of a telephone will ever be interested in examining the connection itself. Does the connection between two telephones have properties that the user cares about? Certainly: it has a start time, and end time, and a cost. These are not properties of either phone, but of the phone call itself.

It is also not true that dialing always yields a destination telephone: the line may be busy, or the call may fail for some other reason. So, we will refine the statement even further:

> "A telephone number is a key that, when dialed on an originating telephone, may yield a connection to a destination telephone."

This statement is much closer to being a useful abstraction than what we started with. However, to really understand what it means, we have to define the other abstractions it depends on. For example:

> "A Connection represents a logical connection between two or more telephones."

1.1.1 What is not in the abstraction?

The things that are *not* in an abstraction are as important as the things that *are* in the abstraction. The telephone number abstraction does not assume that phone numbers have any particular number of digits; does not preclude nondigit characters in the phone number; does not assume that there is a one-to-one correspondence between telephones and telephone numbers; and does not make any statement about how the connection between telephones is actually established.

By keeping the abstraction as small as possible—subject to the constraint that it is still useful—we make it as general as possible. We increase the odds that a future unforeseen change to the phone system will not force us to break the abstraction, although implementations may change. For instance, the advent of cellular phones or the addition of new keys to the standard telephone set would not break this abstraction.

1.1.2   If in doubt, leave it out

If you are unsure whether a particular concept should be in the abstraction, it is usually safer to leave it out than to include it. This is because an error of omission can normally be repaired in an upwardly compatible way—often by adding a new member function to a class. It is much easier to grow an interface than to shrink it. On the other hand, *removing* a member function usually cannot be done compatibly, since there may be user code that calls the removed member function.

1.2   Relationships between abstractions

As part of the initial design process, you should ask yourself a series of questions about how your abstractions interact with one another. This is not meant to be a formal checklist. Depending on your particular application, there may be other equally important questions that need to be asked early rather than later. But the questions in this section tend to come up most often.

Asking these questions has another important benefit. Designs are often wrong because the obvious answer to one of these questions was wrong. When you ask yourself these questions, stop at the ones with obvious answers and think a little harder. Is that answer really true? Try to imagine cases where the obvious answer is wrong. If you catch only one place where the obvious answer is wrong, you may have avoided an expensive design error.

1.2.1   Is the relationship one to one, one to many, many to one, or many-to-many?

Consider the relationship between a telephone and a connection. Can more than one connection be associated with a telephone? In general, yes: one of the parties can be on hold. We also consider the inverse question: can more than one telephone be associated with a connection? The answer here is, of course, also yes: that is the whole point of the telephone! While we are on the subject, we should consider whether more than two telephones can be associated with a connection. The answer, perhaps surprisingly, is also yes: conference calling involves having three or more parties on the line at the same time. The relationship between telephones and connections is many to many.

As another example, consider the relationship between a phone number and a billing address. A single phone number is billed only to one customer and therefore to one address. However, the same address can have two or more phones that are billed to it. This is a many to one relationship (many telephones to a single billing address).

1.2.2 How many is "many"?

If the connection is many to one or many to many, think a little about how many objects are implied by "many". A precise number is usually not necessary (or even desirable). Instead, you should understand whether "many" means:

- Two (or some other constant number);

- Some constant range; for example, if one of the abstractions is "days of the week," there can be at most seven such objects in a relationship with any other object;

- Some variable range, and if variable, about how many (tens, hundreds, millions).

Be careful: good abstractions often end up being used in ways their inventors never dreamed of. If you assume that "many" will never be more than a few tens and therefore use a quadratic algorithm in your implementation, your users will get a nasty surprise when they use it with thousands of objects.

1.2.3 How can the relationship change over time?

Must the existence of the relationship be specified when the involved objects are created, or can objects enter into the relationship after they are created?

Certainly a telephone number can exist without being associated with a Connection; but a Connection must have at least one telephone number associated with it at any time. What about the phone on the other end of the line? Must it be supplied when the Connection is created, or will it be added after? To put it another way, can a Connection to only one phone ever exist? Does the act of picking up the phone (but not dialing) open a Connection?

Answering this requires an understanding of the applications using these objects. We need to know enough about telephony to decide whether those applications will need access to a Connection that is still in the process of being set up or torn down. For the sake of this discussion, we assume that such a Connection would be useful; for instance, billing software might need to access it to record the charges for a call after it is completed. This means that the called party will be added to the Connection set up by the originator of the call.

This model also extends nicely to three way (conference) calls. These calls are not set up all at once, they are set up over time. Each time a new party is added to the call, they join the existing connection.

At this point we realize that we have to refine the executive summary of Connection on page 9. That summary implies that every Connection is between two or more phones. We now see that this is not quite right: we are really interested in a group of *one or more* phones that are talking to each other across the phone network. So we might rephrase this executive summary to say:

> "A Connection represents a group of one or more phones in communication with each other over the telephone network."

This refinement of the abstraction, based on our increased understanding of it, is a normal occurrence. In this case, the name "Connection" still makes sense; that is not always true, and you should be prepared to change the name of the abstraction if the old name no longer describes it adequately.

1.2.4   Is the relationship Is-A, Has-A, or Uses-A?

Different abstractions relate to each other in different ways. The three most common kinds of relationship can be summarized as the *is-a*, *has-a*, and *uses-a* relationships.

The *is-a* relationship

The *is-a* relationship holds for two classes if the objects described by one class belong to the set of objects described by the other, more general, class

(for example, a `Studebaker` *is-a* `Car`.)

The *is-a* relationship is also known as *subtyping*. The subtype is a specialization of some more general type (known as the *supertype*); an object of the subtype *is* also an object of the supertype. These terms are borrowed from Smalltalk. Many C++ programmers will use the C++ equivalents: *derived class* instead of *subtype*, and *base class* instead of *supertype*.

As another example, consider the relationship between a "Push button telephone" and a "Telephone." Every object that is a push button telephone is also a telephone. The set of push button telephones is a subset of the set of telephones (Fig. 1.1).

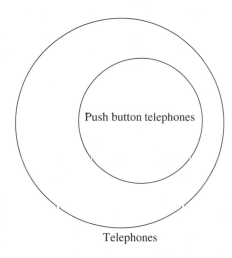

Push button telephones

Telephones

Figure 1.1: A Push button phone *is-a* Telephone

The *is-a* relationship is expressed in C++ by using public inheritance; class `Push_button_phone` would be derived from class `Telephone`:

```
class Telephone {
        // Telephone stuff...
};

class Push_button_phone : public Telephone {
        // Push_button_phone stuff ...
};
```

The subtype (or derived class) can extend the supertype (or base class); a push button telephone may be able to do things that other telephones cannot do. But a subtype should never *restrict* the supertype (e.g., by making a member function that is public in the base class private in the derived class); there should be nothing a telephone can do that a push button telephone cannot do. (If that were the case, push button telephones would not be a subset of telephones.)

The *has-a* relationship

The *has-a* relationship implies containment; a thing *has* another thing if it (conceptually) contains that thing. A telephone contains a speaker and microphone; a push button telephone contains a keypad.

The difference here is that neither object in the relationship is a specialization of the other; instead, one object is a part of the other. A `Push_button_phone` is not a `Keypad`; rather, a `Push_button_phone` *has-a* `Keypad`.

The has-a relationship in C++ is most commonly implemented by having the contained object as a data member of the containing object. However, this need not be the case. The fact that a `Keypad` is *conceptually* contained in a `Push_button_phone` does not mean that the *implementation* must use physical containment. In fact, there are often good reasons for not doing so (as we shall see in Chapter 3); one benefit of data abstraction is that the implementation of an object does not have to match the exact structure of the abstraction. Such decisions should not be a primary concern at this point, since we are still dealing with abstract relationships, not implementation details.

The *uses-a* relationship

The *uses-a* relationship is the most general: neither object is a kind of the other object, and neither object contains the other object. Instead, the two objects will simply communicate with each other at some point in the program. In our telephone example, the telephone and the connection have a *uses-a* relationship.

Objects that *use* each other normally communicate with each other by calling each other's member functions, although other ways of communication (e.g., by shared memory or through some other message passing mechanism) might also be used.

1.2.5   Is the relationship one way or two way?

Given a relationship between two objects, can each object determine what the other one is? That is, if a relationship exists between a Telephone and a Connection, can we get the Telephone from the Connection and vice versa? The answers to these questions can have a fundamental impact on the performance of programs using the abstraction.

A one way relationship can be implemented with regular C++ pointers. Given one of the objects, you get to the other by following the pointer. Reversing this process (finding the object(s) that point at the current object) is harder; it usually involves searching through a large set of objects, examining each one to see if it points at the current object. Depending on the circumstances, this may be not so bad, very expensive, or downright impossible.

A two way relationship is much easier to use: given either object, you can directly get at the other. However, a two way relationship is more expensive to set up. Both objects have to be modified in some way; the two way relationship probably takes more space; and it is more expensive at run time, particularly if the relationships change over time. Changing a one way relationship probably involves changing one pointer. Changing a two way relationship may involve changing three or more pointers, since adding a new relationship between two objects may break some existing relationships. One-way relationships will be faster and smaller than two way relationships and will be easier to program, but they restrict what users of the abstractions will be able to do. This is one of the most common places where implementation issues can (and should) affect the design.

In the case of our telephones, the relationship between a telephone and a connection will almost certainly be two way: given either phone, we would like to be able to get to the phone on the other end of the connection. The alternative of going through every telephone in existence to see if it is connected to the same connection as we are is not practical.

Often the choice is not so clear cut. Consider a compiler that represents expressions as trees, so that a = b + c is represented as the tree in Fig. 1.2. Is the relationship between a node in such a tree and its children one way or two way? There are real performance advantages to keeping the relationship one way; and programs, in practice, may be able to get away with it. For instance, if each tree is walked top-down whenever it is processed, it may be unnecessary to have parent pointers in the tree.

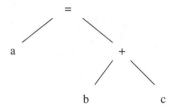

Figure 1.2: An expression tree

1.2.6   Can the relationship hold more than once between two objects?

Given a relationship between two objects, can that relationship hold more than once between the *same* two objects? For instance, the "Father" relationship can hold at most once between two objects: one either is or is not the father of the other. The idea of "he's my father twice" makes no sense. The "article references book" relationship, however, might hold more than once if a single article contained two or more citations of the same book.

1.2.7   Is the relation required?

For every object, must there be at least one object for which the relationship holds? For example, if you have an Employee class, must the *reports-to* relationship hold for each employee? What about the chairperson of the board? Does your class structure support the notion of the chairperson reporting to the board as a whole, or might it be easier to have the chairperson report to no one (or to himself or herself)?

1.3   Worrying about the boundary conditions

You may wonder why we worry about the case of the chairperson of the board. After all, most employees are not the chairperson of the board. Is this special case worth worrying about so early in the design?

Boundary conditions are the places where fundamental assumptions about the abstraction often fail. These questions help to focus your attention on those assumptions. Is each assumption valid? Under which cases does the assumption not hold? Is there a reasonable approach to handling the cases where the assumption does not hold? For instance, if you assume that every employee reports to another employee, when can that assumption be false? What are the consequences in that case?

These boundary conditions are a common source of bugs, and these bugs tend to be discovered late in the game. Rather than wait for such discoveries, these questions are intended to make you think about the boundary conditions earlier on. That is not to say that the exact semantics of every boundary condition need to be set in concrete at this stage in the design. As the design progresses, and you get a better understanding of the issues and problems, you may change your mind about how to handle the chairperson of the board. But you will have identified that particular boundary condition up front, rather than discovering it in system test or in the field.

1.4   Designing with CRC cards

CRC cards (designed by Beck and Cunningham[1]) are a tool that can help in the early part of the design process, when the designers are picking the objects and trying to understand how those objects relate to one another.

The idea is simple and low tech. When a group of people are getting together to do the high level design, they create an index card for each potential class. On the card, they write the name of the class, its main responsibilities, and the classes that it interacts with (its *collaborators*).

The designers can then use these cards to role-play various scenarios. Each participant takes the role of one or more of the objects, and describes the actions taken by his or her object(s) in response to requests from other objects. Based on this role-playing, the responsibilities and collaborators of the classes may be refined (and noted on the cards). Based on the discussions, the group may decide that certain class names are imprecise or confusing and suggest better ones.

The limited space on the cards encourages simple abstractions—complex abstractions are hard to describe on a single index card. The cards also help to identify groups of classes that are candidates for inheritance. Proposed groups can be laid out on a table, and cards representing individual classes can be moved back and forth between groups as the discussion progresses.

All of this role playing and anthropomorphization can get pretty off the wall at times—but this also helps the brainstorming process by encouraging

---

[1]Beck, K., Cunningham, W., "A Laboratory for Teaching Object-Oriented Thinking", *Proceedings OOPSLA '89*, SIGPLAN Notices, Vol. 24, No. 10 (October 1989).

people to say things that they might have "thought better about" in a more formal setting. While most off-the-wall comments may be dead ends, there may be one or two real breakthroughs that would not have been discovered in the traditional, formal design review.

CRC cards are no substitute for a more complete document (that is, the contract) that describes the behavior of a class in detail. Their main utility is in the initial phases of the design: they help in getting the high level ideas right, and they help the designers understand and identify the important issues earlier rather than later.

Consider also using Post-It™ notes: they cannot be shuffled like index cards, but you can stick them on a wall, while preserving the ability to rearrange them.

1.5   In short

- Designing the abstraction and designing the implementation should be two separate, but related, activities.

- What is *not* in an abstraction is as important as what is *in* the abstraction.

- If in doubt, leave it out. Missing functionality can usually be added without breaking compatibility, but removing existing functionality will cause code to break.

- Thoroughly examine and document the key assumptions in your design.

- Iterate on your design.

- Consider the boundary conditions.

- Use CRC cards in the initial stages of your design.

1.6   Questions

1. What other abstractions need to be defined for our telephone number abstraction to make sense?

2. What should happen if an attempt to dial a phone fails for some reason (perhaps the line is busy)? How might our abstraction model this case?

3. Our Connection class assumes that at least one telephone is attached to every Connection. Consider changing this so that a Connection is created with no telephones attached. How would a call be originated in this case? Does this make the abstraction simpler or more complicated?

4. Identify the pairwise *is-a* relationships between these groups of people:

   - biologist;
   - criminal;
   - person;
   - scientist;
   - vivisectionist.

5. Is the relationship between Child and Father one to one, one to many, or many to many? What terms and assumptions have to be clarified for you to answer this question?

Chapter 2

Classes

The most important part of class design is having a clear understanding of the abstraction presented by the class: who it interacts with and what its responsibilities are. That was the focus of the last chapter. Once you have a handle on the abstraction, the next step is the detailed design and implementation of the class itself. This chapter will talk about some of the most common practices—and bugs—involved in that process.

2.1 Constructors

There is more to a constructor than meets the eye. In addition to executing the code written by the programmer, a constructor definition can invoke other constructors to initialize the object's base class parts and data members. The compiler can also insert constructor calls where no explicit call appears in the source—for example, when an implicit conversion is invoked. We will look at some common mistakes involving constructors; some of these cause programs to run slower, while others introduce bugs.

Keep the differences between *initialization* and *assignment* in mind as you read this chapter (see the Review on the next page). You should also be careful not to confuse the terms *default constructor* (a constructor that requires no arguments, either because it was declared with no arguments or has all of its arguments defaulted) and *default copy constructor* (a copy constructor that is created by the compiler).

Review: Initialization and assignment

In C++, an initialization occurs when a new object is created; an assignment changes the value of an existing object (no new object is created.)

```
Thing t = x; // Initialization (new Thing created)
t = x; // Assignment (value of existing Thing changed)
```

Initializations are performed by constructors. Assignments are performed by operator=.

One kind of initialization is special in C++: the initialization of an object using the value of another object of that class. A constructor that performs this initialization is called a *copy constructor* and normally takes the form X::X(const X&).

```
// A complex number class:
class Complex {
// details omitted
public:
    Complex(double, double);
    Complex(const Complex&); //Copy constructor
};
```

If you do not declare a copy constructor, the compiler will create one for you. This *default* copy constructor will initialize each data member of the class by copying its counterpart in the original.

The compiler will automatically generate calls to the copy constructor when objects of the class are passed by value to a function. The temporary objects that are created will be destroyed (by a call to the destructor) when the function returns:

```
double abs(Complex); // arg passed by value, not reference
Complex c(0.0,1.0);
double d = abs(c);
```

abs will actually be passed a *copy* of c; the copy is created by a call to Complex::Complex(const Complex&). After abs returns, the copy will be destroyed by calling the Complex destructor (if there is one).

2.1.1   Does the default copy constructor do the right thing?

Whenever you write a new class, ask yourself whether the default copy constructor and assignment will do the right thing. If not, you will have to declare and define your own.

The default copy constructor for a class will usually (but not always) do the right thing if the entire state of the object is stored in the object. Consider this implementation of a `Complex` number class, which stores the state of the `Complex` number as two `doubles`:

```
class Complex {
private:
    double real;
    double imag;
public:
    Complex(double r, double i) : real(r), imag(i) {}
// details omitted
};
```

Since we have not explicitly declared a copy constructor, we get the default copy constructor, which copies the two data members. That is the right behavior for this class.

On the other hand, suppose we had a `String` class that contained a `char*` that pointed to the characters in the `String`:

```
// In String.h:
class String {
private:
    char* data;
public:
    String(const char* cp = "");
    ~String() { delete [] data; }
};

// In String.c:
String::String(const char* cp)
 : data(new char[strlen(cp)+1]) {
    strcpy(data,cp);
}
```

The default copy constructor for `String` would just copy the `data` pointer, leaving us with two `String` objects pointing at the same memory. This is not right, since the first `String` to be destroyed would delete that memory; the remaining `String` would be left pointing at the deleted memory.

If the default behavior is not right, we must explicitly declare and define the copy constructor:

```
// In String.h:
class String {
private:
    char* data;
public:
    String(const char* = "");
    String(const String&);
    ~String() { delete [] data; }
};

// In String.c:
String::String(const String& s)
: data(new char[strlen(s.data)+1]) {
    strcpy(data,s.data);
}
```

This ensures that each `String` has its own private copy of the data.

We also cannot use the default copy constructor if some extra processing must take place whenever any object of the class is created. Suppose we have a class `File` that represents a file descriptor; that is, a handle that can be used to perform I/O on that file. Applications may wish to know how many `Files` exist at a given time (perhaps to avoid hitting a limit on the number of open file descriptors). This is easily done by having the `File` class maintain a count of currently existing `File` objects. Each `File` constructor increments the count, and each destructor decrements it:

```
// In File.h:
class File {
    static int open_files;
// details omitted
public:
    File(const String& filename, const String& modes);
    File(const File&);
    ~File();
    static int existing() { return open_files; }
};
```

```
// In File.c:
int File::open_files = 0;

File::File(const String& filename, const String& modes) {
    ++open_files;
    // other details omitted
}

File::~File() {
    --open_files;
    // other details omitted
}
```

The static member function `File::existing()` will return a count of the number of existing `File` objects.

For a scheme like this to work, *every* `File` constructor must update the count. The default copy constructor will not do this, so we must write our own:

```
File::File(const File& f) {
    ++open_files;
    // other details omitted
}
```

There is no one general rule that will tell you whether the default copy constructor will work. One rule of thumb is to look especially hard at classes that contain pointers. If the pointed-at objects "belong" to the class object, the default copy constructor is probably wrong, since it will just copy the pointer and not the objects.

2.1.2   Don't ignore copy constructors

Do not fall into the trap of ignoring these issues simply because your own code never calls the copy constructor. Remember that any user of your class can call the copy constructor, either by explicitly creating a new object or by passing an object by value to a function. If, for some reason, it really is too hard to implement a copy constructor for a class, then declare the copy constructor as private, but do not supply a definition:

```
class Cant_be_copied {
private:
    Cant_be_copied(const Cant_be_copied&); // No definition
// details omitted
};
```

By doing this, you at least make sure that code that inadvertently calls the copy constructor will not compile (if it is user code) or link (if it is code in a member or friend of the class). That is not great, but it is much better than code that quietly executes a default copy constructor that does the wrong thing.

2.1.3   Initialization of class members

When a data member of a class is itself a class object, avoid using assignment to set the member's initial value:

```
class Employee {
private:
    String name;
public:
    Employee(const String&);
};

// Slow constructor:
Employee::Employee(const String& n) {
    name = n;
}
```

The constructor will produce the correct result, but it is slower than it needs to be. When an Employee is created, the name member will first be *initialized* using the default String constructor, and then its value will be changed by the *assignment* in the body of the Employee constructor. This is two operations, when one would have sufficed: we can explicitly *initialize* the name member with the right value by using the *initialization syntax* (see the Review on the next page):

```
Employee::Employee(const String& n)
: name(n) {
}
```

Review: Member initialization

By default, before the body of a constructor is executed, all the members of the object are initialized using the default (no argument) constructors. Members that have no constructor have an undefined initial value.

The author of the constructor definition can change this behavior by supplying, after the parenthesis that closes the argument list in the constructor definition, a colon followed by a list of initializers. Each initializer consists of a name and an argument list. Each name is the name of a member or base class of the class being constructed, and each argument list specifies the arguments to the constructor for that member:

```
class String {
public:
    String();
    String(const String&);
    // details omitted
};

class Employee {
private:
    String name;
public:
    Employee(const String&);
};

Employee::Employee(const String& nm)
: name(nm) {
// ...
```

This code tells the compiler to initialize the **name** member with a call to

```
String::String(nm);
```

Members that are of built-in types can also be initialized using this syntax; the argument-list must be a single expression that specifies the initial value.

This constructor does one `String` operation (an initialization), while the original version did two (an initialization followed by an assignment). On my machine, this change cuts the execution time of the `Employee` constructor by about 30 percent.

When you write a constructor definition, stop after the parenthesis that closes the formal arguments list, and see how many of the members of the structure can be initialized using the constructor initialization syntax. You will often find that all of the members can be so initialized, and by the time you get to the body of the constructor, there is nothing left to do! This is a good sign: your constructor has initialized all of its members with the correct initial values.

Members that are not class objects

The initialization syntax can also be used to initialize data members that are not class objects:

```
class Employee {
private:
    String name;
    int     salary;
public:
    Employee(const String&, int);
};

Employee::Employee(const String& n, int sal)
: name(n), salary(sal) {
}
```

Since built-in types have no constructors, initializing the integer member `salary` using the initialization syntax is no faster than using assignment, but the code is easier to read if we initialize all of the data members in the same way.

Order of member initialization

According to the rules of C++, the members of a class are initialized in the order they are listed in the class declaration, *not* in the definition of the constructor. Usually the initialization order is not important, but it matters in some circumstances—for instance, if one of the members is initialized using the value of one of the other members.

Consider an `Employee` class that contains both the name of an `Employee` and an identification number:

```
class Employee {
    String     name;
    long       id;
public:
    Employee(const char* name);
    Employee(long id);
// details omitted
};
```

There are two constructors, one that takes the name of the employee, and one that takes the identification number. Each constructor will look up the missing piece of information in an employee directory.

Here is one (incorrect) attempt at the constructor definitions:

```
extern String lookup_employee(long);
extern long lookup_employee(const String&);

Employee::Employee(const char* n)
: name(n), id(lookup_employee(name)) {
}

Employee::Employee(long i)
: id(i), name(lookup_employee(id)) { // Run time error
}
```

The second constructor compiles but does not work. Since the **name** member appears in the class declaration before the id member, it is always initialized first—even though the initialization of id was written first in the constructor definition! This means that `lookup_employee` is called before `id` is initialized—so its argument will be random garbage. In this case, the problem is easy to fix: use the incoming argument instead of the class member:

```
Employee::Employee(long i)
: id(i), name(lookup_employee(i)) { // OK
}
```

It is not always that easy; in some cases, you may have to rearrange the class definition. If the order of the members is significant, make sure you document this fact in the header file, so that a later reordering of the class declaration does not cause some constructors to fail.

It may seem counterintuitive for the compiler to ignore the order in which the initializers appear in the constructor definition, but this is a consequence of the fact that C++ requires all objects to be destroyed in the reverse of their construction order. If the constructor definition specified the construction order, then the destructor definition would have to look at the constructor definition to figure out the order in which to destroy the members. This would pose a problem for the compiler implementor, since the constructor and destructor may be defined in different files. Even worse, there may be two or more constructors, and there is no guarantee that their definitions will list the members in the same order. The *class declaration*, however, must be available to both files, and it must be consistent (otherwise the behavior of the entire program is undefined); so the class declaration determines the order of construction and destruction of members.

Reference class members

If any nonstatic data member of a class is a reference, every constructor for that class must use the initialization syntax, since every reference must be explicitly initialized:

```
class Payroll_entry {
private:
    Employee& emp;
public:
    Payroll_entry(Employee&);
};

Payroll_entry::Payroll_entry(Employee& e)
{ // Compile time error: ''emp'' must be initialized
}
```

Why might you want emp to be an Employee& instead of an Employee*? In addition to the syntax differences, making emp a reference instead a pointer restricts its use in two ways:

- emp must be bound to an employee when it is created (there is no "0" or "null" reference);

- Once it is bound to an employee, emp can never be changed to refer to another employee.

By making `emp` a reference, we are arranging for the compiler to issue a compile time type error if we attempt to do something that violates either of these rules. The use of a reference instead of a pointer affects only the compile time checking; the generated code will be the same either way.

2.2   Assignment

Like the copy constructor, the C++ compiler will build an assignment operator for your class if you do not declare one. The default assignment operator will assign each of the data members. The default assignment operator will generally work or not work for the same reasons that the default copy constructor works or does not work. If the default copy constructor is wrong, the default assignment operator is almost certainly wrong also (and vice versa).

Assignment operators and copy constructors often have a lot of logic in common. There are three main differences:

- The assignment operator must work correctly when an object is assigned to itself;

- Each call to the assignment operator overwrites an existing value. If that value was using resources external to the object those resources may have to be freed;

- The assignment operator can return a value.

Here are the copy constructor and assignment operator for the `String` class:

```
String::String(const String& s)
 : data(new char[strlen(s.data)+1]) {
     strcpy(data,s.data);
}
```

```
const String&
String::operator=(const String& s) {
    if (&s != this) {
        delete [] data;
        data = new char[strlen(s.data)+1];
        strcpy(data,s.data);
    }
    return *this;
}
```

Let's look more closely at this assignment operator. The comparison of **&s** and **this** is to guard against code that does

```
String s;
s = s;
```

Without this test, an assignment of a **String** to itself would delete the data of that **String** and then try to copy the just-deleted data. Whenever you write an assignment operator, consider the possibility that the operand and the object being assigned to are the same object, and make sure your code will do the sensible thing in that case (which is usually nothing). You might not expect anyone to write

```
s = s;
```

but code that uses pointers or references might have the same effect.

Once we are sure that we are dealing with two different objects, the assignment operator (unlike the copy constructor) should release any resources that held the old value. (That is what the **delete** is for.) After that, the assignment operator usually does the same thing as the copy constructor, except that the assignment operator returns a value. The common logic is often put into a private member function that is called by the copy constructor and assignment operators; for this class, the common logic is a single function call, so we just duplicate the call.

2.2.1   Return value of operator=

Assignment operators should return a const reference to the assigned-to object. This allows users to write code like:

```
Complex x,y;
// ...
x = y = Complex(0,0);
```

An overloaded operator has the same precedence and associativity as its built-in version. = is right associative, so the assignment

```
y = Complex(0,0);
```

is evaluated first, and its result is then assigned to x.

By returning a const reference, we prevent an assignment from being used as an lvalue:

```
(a=b)=c;
```

Not only does this look strange, but its behavior is surprisingly subtle. For instance, consider what happens if a and c are references to the same location.

There is one drawback to having assignment return a value: it takes some code to return a value, even when it is ignored:

```
a = b; // Return value unused
```

This is almost always acceptable in practice. The extra code is usually a single machine instruction (remember that we return a *reference*, which is really just a pointer, not a whole new object). Usually the performance impact of a single instruction is insignificant. If it is significant, the assignment operator should probably be made inline; in that case a decent optimizer should be able to eliminate the instruction when the result of the assignment is unused.

2.3   Public data

Consider this complex number class:

```
class Complex {
public:
    double real;
    double imag;
    Complex(double r, double i) : real(r), imag(i) {}
    // Other stuff omitted
};
```

This class may work, but its interface is badly flawed. The problem is the two public data members: **real** and **imag**. This interface promises that the real and imaginary parts of a `Complex` are stored, as `doubles`, in the `Complex` object. Since user code accesses the public data members directly:

```
Complex c(3.0,4.0);
double d = c.real;
c.imag = 0.0;
```

it is hard to change the implementation to store the information in a different form or in a different place.

Suppose that in a later release we wished to change the implementation of `Complex` (but not the interface) to store the information in polar form instead of Cartesian form. (Perhaps we have some critical algorithm that works best if the numbers are stored in polar form.) If the Cartesian coordinates are public data, we are stuck: we must either break users' code or maintain *both* the polar and Cartesian forms in every `Complex` object.·

We would not have had this problem if we had avoided public data in the first place:

```
class Complex {
private:
    double real_d;
    double imag_d;
public:
    Complex(double r, double i) : real_d(r), imag_d(i) {}
    double real() const { return real_d; }
    double imag() const { return imag_d; }
    void real(double r) { real_d = r; }
    void imag(double i) { imag_d = i; }

    // Other stuff omitted
};
```

While the interface specifies that a `Complex` can yield real and imaginary parts as `doubles`, the fact that those `doubles` are stored in the object in that form is a private implementation detail. User code gets the values by calling member functions, not by referring to data members:

```
Complex c(3.0,4.0);
double d = c.real();
c.imag(0.0);
```

The only difference to the users is that they have to type an extra two characters (the parentheses) to get the value. Because `Complex::real` is an inline function, the generated code should be the same—there is no performance penalty for wrapping the access in an inline function. Changes to the values can also be wrapped in inline functions without penalty.

Now that our class has no public data, it is easy to change the interface so that the information is stored in a different form:

```
// File Complex.h:
class Complex {
private:
    double r;
    double theta;
public:
    Complex(double re, double im); // No longer inline
    double real() const { return r*sin(theta); }
    double imag() const { return r*cos(theta); }
    void real(double); // No longer inline
    void imag(double); // No longer inline

    // Other details omitted
};

// File Complex.c:
Complex::Complex(double re, double im)
    . r(sqrt( re*re + im*im )),
      theta(atan2(im,re)) {
}

// ``real(double)'' and ``imag(double)''
//    left as an exercise
```

User code must be recompiled, and the performance will be affected, but the interface has not changed. Programs that used to work will still work.

We could also change the implementation to store the information in a different place:

```
class Complex_rep {
private:
    friend class Complex;
    double real_d;
    double imag_d;
    Complex_rep(double r, double i): real_d(r), imag_d(i){}
};
```

```
class Complex {
private:
    Complex_rep*  rep;
public:
    Complex(double r, double i)
    : rep(new Complex_rep(r,i)) {}
    ~Complex() { delete rep; }
// details omitted
};
```

Chapter 3 discusses some reasons for doing this.

2.3.1   Representation invariants

Public data also makes it almost impossible to enforce a *representation invariant* on your class. A representation invariant is a predicate that is guaranteed to be true for every fully constructed object of the class.

For example, suppose we had a `Rational` class that represented a rational number as a pair of integers (a numerator and a denominator):

```
class Rational {
private:
    int num_d;
    int denom_d;
public:
    Rational(int n, int d);
    int num() const { return num_d; }
    int denom() const { return denom_d; }
    void num(int n) { num_d = n; }
    void denom(int); // Change denominator
};
```

Let's assume that it will make our algorithms simpler and faster if our class has a representation invariant that the denominator (`denom_d`) is never zero. Every operation that can set the value of the denominator checks the proposed new denominator; if it is zero, it raises an error[1]:

---

[1] If you are using a compiler that supports exceptions, an exception (see Chapter 10) should be thrown instead of aborting.

```
static void
check_zero(int d) {
    if (d == 0) {
        cerr <<  "Zero denominator in Rational\n";
        abort();
    }
}

Rational::Rational(int n, int d)
: num_d(n),
  denom_d(d) {
    check_zero(d);
}

void
Rational::denom(int d) {
    check_zero(d);
    denom_d = d;
}
```

Since the invariant is enforced by these two functions, the rest of the **Rational** member functions need not worry about the possibility of a zero denominator. If the denominator were a public data member, there would be no way to enforce the invariant, user code could set the denominator to zero at any time. *Every* operation on a **Rational** would have to allow for that possibility.

The moral: avoid public data. Public data prevents you from changing the implementation of your classes to store that information in a different form or in a different place; and it makes it impossible to enforce a representation invariant.

2.4   Implicit type conversions

Every implicit type conversion (see the Review on the next page) gives the compiler permission to quietly rewrite your code. For this reason, implicit conversions should be provided and used sparingly: code that has lots of implicit conversions can be hard to understand. Furthermore, the more implicit conversions you have, the greater the odds are that a given function call will be ambiguous, requiring explicit casts to disambiguate the call. In this section, we will demonstrate some of the problems that often occur in

Review: Implicit type conversions

An *implicit type conversion* from type F to type T is declared by either:

- A T constructor that can take a single F argument (including functions with defaults, such as `T::T(F,int=0)`)

- An `operator` T conversion function that is a member of F.

If no declaration exactly matches the actual arguments supplied to a function call, the compiler will attempt to resolve the function call by applying implicit type conversions to the arguments. For each function declaration with the given name that is in scope, the compiler attempts to match the arguments to the declaration by applying at most one user-defined implicit conversion to each argument. If exactly one function is a match, the conversions will be silently applied and the function called; otherwise it is a compile time error.

```
class Rational {
public:
// ...
    Rational(int,int);
    operator double();
};

double sqrt(double);

main() {
    Rational r(4,1);
    double sq = sqrt(r);
};
```

`r` is implicitly converted to a `double`, just as if the user had written:

```
        double dval = r.operator double();
        double sq = sqrt(dval);
```

code that uses implicit conversions. We will also suggest some guidelines for when implicit conversions should be used.

2.4.1   Single-argument constructors

The fact that a single-argument constructor specifies an *implicit* conversion is awkward, since a single-argument constructor is often the obvious choice for *explicit* construction. Such constructors should be *used* implicitly only if they are (conceptually) converting the same information from one form to another. An implicit conversion tends to be confusing if the new object is (conceptually) different from the constructor argument. There is a gray area between these two cases, so let's look at some examples.

```
class String {
// details omitted
public:
    String(const char* = "");
};

void print_heading(const String&);
// ...
print_heading("Annual Report");
```

The call to `print_heading` invokes an implicit conversion from `char*` to `String`; but a `String` and a `char*` are conceptually two ways to represent the same abstraction, so the conversion is reasonable.

```
class Rational {
// details omitted
public:
    Rational(long num = 0, long denom = 1);
};

int operator==(const Rational&, const Rational&);

int
nonzero(const Rational& r) {
    return r == 0;
}
```

This case is less clear-cut but perhaps still defensible. The 0 is implicitly converted to a `Rational` (the second argument to the `Rational` constructor is defaulted to 1). As the code is written, however, the comparison looks cheaper than it actually is. The explicit version:

```
int
nonzero(const Rational& r) {
    return r == Rational(0,1);
}
```

gives a better indication of the actual cost of the function and suggests this optimization:

```
int
nonzero(const Rational& r) {
    static const Rational zero(0,1);
    return r == zero;
}
```

This avoids the expense of creating and destroying a new `Rational` at each call to `nonzero`. Only a very astute programmer would have figured this out from an inspection of the original version of this function.

Here is another example:

```
#include <stdlib.h>
// Random number generator:
class Random_gen {
// details omitted
public:
    Random_gen(long seed);
};

void play_game(Random_gen);

main(int argc, char* argv[]) {
    if (argc > 1)
        play_game(atoi(argv[0])); // Confusing
}
```

This implicit conversion should not have been used. An object that generates random numbers is not just a different form of the seed; it is a completely different object that happens to use a `long` in its constructor. The fact that the value from `atoi` is not actually passed to `play_game` is very easy to miss. The code should be rewritten to invoke the constructor explicitly:

```
int
main(int argc, char* argv[]) {
    if (argc > 1) {
        Random_gen gen(atoi(argv[0]));
        play_game(gen); // Better
    }
    // ...
}
```

This is as fast as the previous version (the code for the constructor call is generated whether you write it or not) but is less subtle.

2.4.2   Conversion operators

Classes with more than one conversion operator are much more likely to generate compile time ambiguities when they are used. For example, this class has just one conversion operator:

```
class String {
    char* rep;
public:
    String(const char* = "");
    operator const char*() const { return rep; }
    // Other stuff omitted
};
```

```
main() {
    String s("hello world");
    cout << s << endl;
}
```

This code works; there is no declared **String** output operator, so the **String** is converted to a **const char***.

Consider what happens if we now add an extra conversion operator to

String:

```
class String {
    char* rep;
public:
    String(const char* = "");
    operator const char*() const { return rep; }
    operator int() const { return atoi(rep); } //Added
    // Other stuff omitted
};
```

This conversion operator looks like it might make things more convenient, since any **String** can be used where an **int** is needed; but the change breaks existing code:

```
main() {
    String s("hello world");
    cout << s << endl; // Compile time error:
                       // ambiguous conversion
}
```

An attempt to output a **String** can now be resolved either by converting the **String** to a **const char*** or to an **int**; so we get a compile time error. To get our code to compile, we have to add an explicit cast:

```
cout << (const char*)s;
```

The presence of two implicit conversions from **String** makes an ambiguity more likely.

This does not mean that there should be no way to convert a **String** to an **int**, only that the conversion should not be implicit:

```
class String {
    char* rep;
public:
    int as_int() { return atoi(rep); }
    // Other stuff omitted
};
```

The conversion of a **String** to an **int** now requires an explicit call of the as_int function:

```
void
process_key_value(const String& key, const String& val) {
    if (numeric_key(key)) {
        int value = val.as_int();
        // ...
```

but that is not a bad thing, since the explicit call makes the behavior of the program easier to understand.

2.4.3   Implicit conversions between built-in types

The rules for implicit conversions when one of the types involved is a class type are stable and well understood. The rules for implicit conversions between the integral built-in types, on the other hand, are subtle and have a history of changing as the language has matured. For instance,

```
void f(long);
void f(int);
main() {
    f('x'); // Which f?
}
```

This is a call to f(int), but this

```
void f(long);
void f(unsigned int);
main() {
    f('x'); // Which f?
}
```

is a compile time error (ambiguous function call). Even if you understand the language rules enough to understand why this is so, the next person to maintain the code may not. It is a good idea to avoid writing code that depends on dark corners of the language, so if you really need to do something different for different integral built-in types, you should provide an exact match for each of the integral built-in types:

```
void output(long);
void output(unsigned long);
void output(int);
void output(unsigned int);
void output(short);
void output(unsigned short);
void output(char);
void output(unsigned char);
void output(signed char);
```

Now, you can be sure that the meaning of

```
unsigned short s;
output(s);
```

is both obvious and not subject to change.

2.5   Overloaded operators: members or nonmembers?

There are two ways to overload operators in C++: the operator can be a member function or it can be a nonmember function. This section will present some guidelines for deciding which alternative to use for a particular operator.

Of course, if you overload an operator to work on a class that is not owned by you, that operator must be a nonmember function: if you do not own the class, you cannot add members to it! The rest of this section assumes that you have the option of making the operator a member.

The choice of member vs. nonmember affects the code that implements the operator; for instance, a member function can refer to **this**, and use the unqualified names of the class members. However, the choice between members and nonmembers also affects the behavior of the operator as seen by the user. If the operator is implemented as a member, *implicit conversions will not be applied to the first (leftmost) operand*. This difference is visible to the user, so it, and not the coding differences, should be the primary criterion for choosing between the member and nonmember forms.

2.5.1   Unary operators

Let's start with an example of a unary operator. Suppose we have a class `Vector` whose objects are constructed from a `Direction` and a `double` magnitude:

```
class Direction {
// details omitted
};

class Vector {
public:
    Vector(const Direction&, double magnitude = 0.0);
};
```

Since the second argument of the `Vector` constructor is defaulted, there is an implicit conversion from `Direction` to `Vector`.

Now suppose that we wish to overload unary `operator-` for a `Vector`. If we make it a nonmember, we can apply the operator to a `Direction`, which will be implicitly converted to a `Vector`:

```
Vector operator-(const Vector&);

main() {
    Direction d;
    Vector v = -d; // Legal: operator-(Vector(d))
}
```

If `operator-` is a member function, the implicit conversion is suppressed:

```
class Vector {
public:
    Vector(const Direction&, double magnitude = 0.0);
    Vector operator-() const;
};

main() {
    Direction d;
    Vector v = -d; // Compile time error
}
```

I consider the suppression of the implicit conversion to be a good thing, since (as we saw in Section 2.4) the use of implicit conversions can make code harder to maintain and understand. For this reason I recommend that unary operators be implemented as member functions when you have the choice.

2.5.2   =, [], (), and ->

According to the language rules, these four operators *must* be members. An attempt to declare one of them a nonmember causes a compile time error:

```
extern int operator=(Complex&, const Complex&);
// Compile time error: operator= must be a member
```

2.5.3   Other binary operators

For the other binary operators, the choice between members and nonmembers should be determined by whether you want to allow implicit conversions on the left operand. For the assignment operators (like +=) suppression of implicit conversions on the left operand is desirable:

```
Complex c;
c += 5;
```

It is hard to imagine a circumstance where c should be implicitly converted to something else before the += operator is applied. If the code successfully compiled, it would not change the value of c; this would be confusing. Making the assignment operators members prevents this, and ensures that their behavior is consistent with the behavior of operator= (which *must* be a member).

For the nonassignment binary operators, however, it can be confusing to suppress implicit conversions on the left operand while allowing them on the right operand. For instance,

```
class Complex {
// details omitted
public:
    Complex(double = 0.0, double = 0.0);
    Complex operator+(const Complex&) const;
};
```

```
main() {
    Complex c(1.0);
    Complex d = c + 1.0; //OK
    Complex e = 1.0 + c; //Compile time error
}
```

Notice that we have added default arguments to the `Complex` constructor. This has the effect of declaring an implicit conversion from `double` to `Complex` (the constructor will be called with the second argument defaulted to `0.0`). The second invocation of `operator+` fails to compile because no suitable declaration is in scope; the compiler will not implicitly convert the left operand to call a member function on it. If `operator+` had been declared a nonmember then both forms would have compiled.

When both operands are inputs to the operation, but neither is affected by the operation, it is usually best to make the operator a nonmember. This ensures that both operands act the same way in the presence of implicit conversions.

The suggestions of this section are summarized in Fig. 2.1.

Operator	Recommended use
All unary operators	member
= () [] ->	*must* be member
+= -= /= *= ^= &= |= ~= %= >>= <<=	member
All other binary operators	nonmember

Figure 2.1: Overloaded operators: members or nonmembers?

2.6   Overloading, defaults, and ellipsis

C++ makes it possible for users to write two expressions that appear to call the same function, but pass arguments that differ in their number or type:

```
f();
f(0);
f(x,y,z);
```

(Of course, this should be done only if the functions are performing the same *abstract* operation on their arguments.) There are three different ways to do this in C++: overload the function, use default arguments, or use the ellipsis notation. There are rules that specify exactly what happens if you use more than one of these methods at once with the same function name. They are subtle and can lead to surprises. Even if you understand all the interactions, it is unlikely that the next person to maintain your code will fully understand what is going on. For any one name, choose one scheme and stick with it.

The ellipsis notation should be used only for functions like `printf` that would otherwise require an infinite—or nearly infinite—number of over-loaded versions. There is no compile time type checking of the variable arguments; and the called function must use the magic macros in `stdarg.h` to get at the variable arguments. If the function gets it wrong, the result is chaos.

Assuming that we have eliminated the ellipsis, the choice between default arguments and overloading is usually easy. Defaults provide multiple ways to call a single function; overloading is appropriate if different functions need to be called.

If one of the alternatives is a degenerate case of the other, and the same implementation will work for both cases, a default is the logical choice. For example, we might have a `String` class that takes a `const char*` argument to its constructor; but we would also like to have a default constructor. A default argument is a convenient way to do this:

```
class String {
// details omitted
public:
    String(const char* = "");
};

String s; // Same as `` String s(""); ''
```

Overloading is used when the various alternatives are conceptually similar, but have different implementations:

```
void print(const Date&);
void print(const Location&);
void print(const Employee&);
```

While the three `print` operations are conceptually the same, they will have different implementations, so overloading must be used.

2.6.1   Defaulted pointer and reference arguments

This little syntax trap comes up when pointer arguments are defaulted:

```
void f(const char*= "");
```

The compiler will see *= as a single token, causing a syntax error. You need a space after the *:

```
void f(const char* = "");
```

Defaulted reference arguments work the same way:

```
const String empty;
void f(const String&= empty); // Syntax error
void f(const String& = empty); // OK
```

2.7   Const

Many C++ programmers' first use of const is to define manifest constants; instead of

```
// C version:
#define BUFF_LENGTH 1024
int buffer[BUFF_LENGTH];
```

the C++ programmer would write

```
// C++ version:
const int BUFF_LENGTH = 1024;
int buffer[BUFF_LENGTH];
```

This has the advantage of allowing the compiler (or some other tool) to know about the name and type of BUFF_LENGTH. There is no penalty in execution time or program size, since the compiler is not required to lay down storage for BUFF_LENGTH if its address is never taken.

However, const is much more than just a way to declare manifest constants. By declaring a "pointer to const," you are declaring that the pointer cannot be used to change the pointed-at object. In this section, we look at some of the ways a pointer (or reference) to const can affect your code.

Remember that making something const (or pointer or reference to const) just invokes extra compile time checking; it does not cause the compiler to generate any extra code.

2.7.1   Const reference arguments

In C++, function arguments are passed by value. This means that a copy of the argument is passed to the called function; changes to that copy do not affect the value in the calling function.

When a class object is passed by value to a function, it gets copied like any other function argument, via a call to the copy constructor. When the function returns, the compiler generates code to destroy the copy (the destructor is called). This copying can get expensive, especially if the called function itself passes the object to other functions. In this case, each top-level call can cause several copies of the object to be constructed and destroyed.

In the vast majority of cases, even though the object is *conceptually* passed by value, the called function does not need its own copy of the object; it can use a *const reference* to the original object:

```
// Correct but slow:
// unneeded copy of the Telephone_number:
void
dial(Telephone_number tn) {
// details omitted
}


// Better: use of a const reference:
void
dial(const Telephone_number& tn) {
// details omitted
}
```

The second version will be faster, as it avoids the overhead of making a copy of the input argument and destroying the copy when the function returns. The use of `const` prevents the called function from inadvertently doing something that would change the value of the object in the calling function.

The use of a reference provides users with some important syntactic sugar: they need not remember which arguments are passed as pointers and which are passed as values. If an argument is conceptually passed by value, the call is written that way; the fact that it is passed by reference is an implementation detail.

2.7.2 Const arguments and const pointers

Different C++ programmers feel differently about `const`. Some see it as an important tool that finds bugs at compile time; others see it as more bother than it is worth and do not use it. If you are writing code that will be used by others, the second alternative is not open to you: even if you do not use `const`, some of the people who use your class will, so you will have to allow for that by declaring things to be `const` when appropriate.

This comes up most often with functions that take pointer arguments. If a function only fetches through a pointer argument—it does not store through it or do anything that changes the pointed-at object—the function declaration should declare the argument as pointer to const:

```
class String {
public:
    String(const char* = "");
// details omitted
};
```

This declaration promises that the `String` constructor never stores through its pointer argument. (An attempt to write such a store in the definition of the `String` constructor would cause a compile time error.) If the `String` constructor had been declared as taking a `char*` instead of a `const char*`, any user who had a pointer to const could not use it to build a `String`:

```
// in String.h:
class String {
public:
    String(char* = ""); // Should be "const char*"
// details omitted
};

// in user code:

main() {
    const char* hello = "hello world";
    String s(hello); // Compile time error:
                     // No acceptable String constructor
}
```

This discussion also applies to functions that take references: if the function will not store through the reference, it should take a const reference. A const reference argument also makes it possible for a reference to an unnamed temporary to be passed to the function:

```
Thing get_a_thing();

void look_at_thing(const Thing&);
void change_thing(Thing&);

look_at_thing(get_a_thing()); // OK
change_thing(get_a_thing()); // Compile time error
```

The call to change_thing generates a compile time error: it is illegal to pass an unnamed temporary to a function as a nonconst reference. This rule was added to C++ because it was felt that a situation in which the called function changed the value of a reference argument that was then discarded by the caller was probably a bug. If this is really what is intended, a named object must be created:

```
Thing t(get_a_thing());
change_thing(t);   // OK
```

Declaring something as pointer to const is a statement about the *pointer*, not about the space being pointed to. The compiler will not ensure that the data being pointed at will not change; it ensures only that it will not change *through that pointer*. The pointed-at object can still be changed by some other means:

```
void
do_callback(const int* ip, void(*callback)()) {
    cout << *ip << endl;
    (*callback)();
    cout << *ip << endl;
}
```

Even though ip is a pointer to const int, there is no guarantee that the same number will be printed twice. For instance,

```
int i = 5;
void
bump_i() {
    ++i;
}
```

```
main() {
    do_callback(&i, bump_i);
}
```

This prints:

```
5
6
```

The callback function changed i between the two prints.

A syntax nit

When we called through the function pointer in do_callback, we explicitly dereferenced the pointer:

```
(*callback)();
```

However, if you just "call" the pointer by applying the () operator to it, that is the same as calling through the pointer:

```
callback();
```

The generated code is the same in both cases.

This is just syntactic sugar, and I suggest you avoid taking advantage of it. When the first form is used, the calls through function pointers are obvious; if the second form is used, you have to realize that the type of the "function" is really "pointer to function." The benefit of having to type a few less keystrokes is not worth the increased subtlety of the resulting code.

2.7.3   Const member functions

Member functions that do not change the value of the object should be declared const (see the Review on the next page).   This allows others to create const objects of your classes and have the compiler check every member function call to make sure the objects will not be changed.

Nonconst member functions on unnamed temporaries

Even though you cannot pass a nonconst reference to an unnamed temporary, as of this writing it is legal to call a nonconst member function on an

Review: Const member functions

A member function may be declared `const` by supplying the `const` keyword after the argument list in both the declaration and definition:

```
// in String.h:
class String {
public:
    // details omitted
    int length() const;
    void capitalize(); // Not const
};

// in String.c:
int
String::length() const {
// details omitted
}

void
String::capitalize() { // Not const
// details omitted
}
```

Only const member functions can be called on const objects:

```
const String s("hello");
int len = s.length(); // OK
s.capitalize(); // Compile time error: nonconst function
                // called on const object

String t("world"); // Not a const String
len = t.length(); // OK
t.capitalize(); // OK
```

In the definition of a const member function, all data members of the object are const, and "`this`" has the type "const pointer to const object," not "const pointer to object."

unnamed temporary:

```
class String {
public:
    void capitalize(); // Not const
};
// ...
String make_up_name();
make_up_name().capitalize(); // OK, but shouldn't be
```

This is an oversight in the language definition that I hope will be corrected by the ISO/ANSI C++ standards committee; in any case, you should not take advantage of it. If you need to call a nonconst member function on an object, the object should be given a name and explicitly defined:

```
String name(make_up_name());
name.capitalize(); // Better
```

This will guarantee that **name** will not be destroyed until the flow of control leaves the block in which it was defined.

Const member functions that change the bits

The C++ language rules ensure that a const member function does not change the state (data members) of the object, unless the const-ness is explicitly cast away. However, some operations that are *conceptually* const might actually change the value of some members; this fact should be an implementation detail that is not visible to the user. These operations should be declared as const, and an explicit cast supplied. In this way, a user can perform an operation on a const object that (conceptually) does not change its value, without having to be aware that the implementation of that operation changes some private data member of the object.

For example, suppose that we are using the version of **Complex** that stores the value in polar form (see page 35). We might wish to cache the Cartesian values when they are computed in order to save the run time cost of recomputing them the next time they are requested. Each object contains a boolean indicating whether the caches are valid:

```
typedef unsigned char Boolean;
class Complex {
private:
    double r, theta;
    double real_cache, imag_cache;
    Boolean real_cache_valid;
    Boolean imag_cache_valid;
public:
    Complex(double real, double imag);
    double real_part() const;
    void   real_part(double);

    double imag_part() const;
    void   imag_part(double);
};
```

The constructor sets the cache bits to zero to indicate that the cache is not valid:

```
#include <math.h>
Complex::Complex(double re, double im)
: r(sqrt( re*re + im*im )),
  theta(atan2(im,re)),
  real_cache_valid(0),
  imag_cache_valid(0)
{}
```

The functions that fetch (but do not set) the values are conceptually const, but they may update the cache:

```
double
Complex::real_part() const {
    if (!real_cache_valid) {
        (double&)real_cache = r*sin(theta);
        (Boolean&)real_cache_valid = 1;
    }
    return real_cache;
}
```

To change data members of an object in a const member function, we must cast away their const-ness. According to the rules of C++, this is legal and will do the right thing as long as the class has a constructor. (If there is no constructor, the behavior of casting away the **const** is undefined; this rule was intended to allow the compiler to put things like **const ints** into ROM.)

2.8   Returning references

Functions can return references. Returning a reference is like returning a pointer; the object being referred to must still exist after the function returns. In particular, you should not return a reference to an automatic, for the same reason that you should not return a pointer to an automatic: the automatic is destroyed when the function returns, leaving a dangling reference.

For example, our **String** assignment operator can return a reference to ***this**, since the assigned-to object will still exist when the assignment is complete. On the other hand, a concatenation function that creates a new **String** should return it by value:

```
String  /* Not String& */
operator+(const String& left, const String& right) {
    String result;
    // build ''result,'' then:
    return result;
}
```

We should not return a reference to **result**, since **result** is destroyed when **operator+** returns. We must return it by value; this will cause a *copy* of **result** to be returned to the caller.

There is a performance penalty here, since we must first build a local copy of the object and then return it (via a call to the copy constructor); but this idiom is so common that many compilers can optimize away the copy.

2.9   Static constructors

Objects with static storage class may be initialized by constructors:

```
static String hello("Hello world");
```

The C++ compilation system is responsible for ensuring that static objects are initialized before they are used. Most compilers implement this by initializing all static objects before **main** begins, but the language rules are worded to allow a dynamic linker to initialize all of the objects in a compilation unit at (dynamic) link time.

The order of initialization of static objects *in* a compilation unit is the order in which they appear in the source:

```
String default_name("foo");
String default_src_file(default_name + ".c");
```

`default_name` is guaranteed to be initialized before `default_src_file`. Static objects in a file will be destroyed in the reverse order, so that `default_src_file` will be destroyed before `default_name`.

The order of initialization *between* files is *not* defined:

```
extern String default_name;
String default_src_file(default_name + ".c"); // Bug!
```

There is no guarantee that `default_name` will we be initialized before `default_src_file`.

There are no easy solutions to this problem. If you have a static object (like `default_src_file`) that has a dependency on a static object in another file, you should try to put both objects in the same file (where their initialization order will be well-defined). If this is impossible, you may have to delay the initialization until **main** executes:

```
extern String default_name;
String* default_src_file = 0;

static void
init_names() {
    default_src_file = new String(default_name + ".c");
    // any other initializations that are required
}

main() {
    init_names();
```

If your code is in a library, and **main** is not available, each routine that uses the object with the dependency may have to check to see if it has been initialized:

```
extern String default_name;
String* default_src_file = 0;
```

```
void
routine_that_uses_name() {
    if (default_src_file == 0)
        default_src_file = new String(default_name+".c");
    // Use default_src_file
```

Avoid "initialization object" schemes that cause code to be executed in every compilation unit that includes a given header file. One side effect of the new templates feature (see Chapter 7) is an increase in the number of compilation units in a given program (since each template is usually instantiated into a separate compilation unit). It is not hard, when using templates, to build programs that contain hundreds of compilation units. A scheme that exacts a run time cost for every compilation unit will be too expensive for such programs.

2.10 In short

- Decide whether the default copy constructor and assignment are right, and reimplement them if necessary.

- Avoid using assignments to initialize members; use the constructor initialization syntax instead.

- When writing an assignment operator, check for the s = s case.

- Avoid public data.

- Declare and use implicit conversions sparingly. Avoid having two or more conversion operators in the same class.

- Unary operators, assignment operators, (), [], and -> should be members; other operators should be nonmembers.

- Use defaults to provide different ways to call the same function; use overloading to provide two or more implementations of the same abstract operation.

- Pass class objects using const references unless the called function needs its own copy of the object.

- Declare pointer arguments as pointer to const when possible. Declare reference arguments as reference to const when possible.

- Declare member functions const when possible.

- The order of initialization of statics across files is undefined.

2.11   Questions

1. The copy constructor `X::X(X)` is illegal in C++. Explain why.

2. Our `String` constructors got space for the data by doing

   ```
   new char[strlen(cp)+1];
   ```

   Since there are only `strlen(cp)` characters in the string, what is the extra byte for?

3. Our `File` class assumes that every `File` object represents a unique file descriptor—copying a `File` creates a new descriptor. Suppose instead that copying a `File` created another object that shared an existing descriptor—so that this copy should not increment the count of existing descriptors. How would you implement the `File` class to support this? (Hint: just having the copy constructor not bump the count is not enough.)

4. A compiler implementor might save on implementation costs by not doing inline expansion: every call to an inline function would generate a real function call. This would be legal C++, but would be a disaster for the users of that compiler. Why?

5. A programmer may want to provide an addition operator for any combination of `doubles` or `Rationals`. Suggest two ways to provide this, and discuss the pros and cons of each.

6. Enhance your solution to the previous question to support `Complex` operands.

7. Implement the functions to set the (Cartesian) real and imaginary portions of our `Complex` class that is implemented using polar coordinates.

8. The routines to set the real and imaginary portions of our `Complex` class return `void`. What other values might it make sense for them to return? Is one of the other answers clearly right? If not, what approach do you recommend?

9. Assume you are using a `String` class that provides an `operator const char*` function:

```
class String {
public:
    operator const char*() const;
    // Other stuff omitted
};
```

Assume further that we have a `remove_blanks` function that squeezes the blanks out of the string pointed to by its `char*` argument:

```
void
remove_blanks(char* cp) {
    char* p = cp;
    while(*p) {
        if (*p != ' ')
            *cp++ = *p;
        ++p;
    }
    *cp = '\0';
}
```

Finally, suppose a user tries to use this function to remove the blanks from a `String`, reasoning that the function can only make the `String` shorter, not longer:

```
String s(" hello  world  ");
remove_blanks((char*)(const char*)s);
```

Is this safe? Why or why not?

10. What is wrong with this class?

```
class Node {
// details omitted
public:
    Node(); //Leaf
    Node(const Node&); //Unary
    Node(const Node&, const Node&); //Binary
};
```

How would you change the interface to fix the problem?

Chapter 3

Handles

One of the main benefits of data abstraction is that the physical structure of an object does not have to reflect its abstract structure. Just because the model that you present to your user looks like it has certain physical properties does not mean you have to implement it that way. As long as the *behavior* of your objects matches the abstract model, you can use any implementation you like.

In particular, if the abstract model specifies that one object "contains" another, your implementation does not have to make the contained object a data member of the containing object. Instead, the containing object can have a *handle* to the representation of the contained object. (The object that implements the representation is usually called the *rep*.) A handle is, conceptually, a pointer to some other C++ object, and it's often implemented as an ordinary C++ pointer. We use the term "handle" because the handle could itself be some other C++ object that provided the same functionality; we'll see some examples of such "smart pointers" in Chapter 7.

Handles can provide several advantages:

- The implementation can support constant-sized objects with variable-sized values.

- The implementation of each object can be bound at run time instead of compile time.

- Changes to the implementation are more likely to require a relink instead of a recompile.

- The implementation of an object can be hidden from prying eyes.

On the down side, handles require extra programming and impose some run time cost.

In this chapter, we'll look at several ways of using handles. We start with a familiar example.

3.1   A String class

A C++ class object always has a constant size, as measured by the `sizeof` operator. However, the representations of the values need not all be the same size; instead, each object can contain a (constant-sized) handle to the (variable-sized) value. When the object is created, its constructor will use `new` to get the space for the value.

The *rep* of our `String` class will be a null terminated sequence of characters on the heap. The `String` object will contain the handle, which will be a `char*`:

```
class String {
private:
    char* rep;
public:
    String(const char* = "");
    ~String();
    String(const String&);
    const String& operator=(const String&);
};
```

Every class that contains a handle implemented as a pointer should contain at least the following functions.

3.1.1   Constructor and Destructor

The constructor of the containing object initializes the handle to point to the rep. For our `String` class, the `String` constructor will create the rep and initialize the pointer to point at it:

```
String::String(const char* c)
: rep(new char[strlen(c)+1]) {
    strcpy(rep,c);
}
```

The `String` destructor will be responsible for deleting the rep:

```
String::~String() {
    delete [] rep;
}
```

3.1.2   Copy constructor

The default copy constructor will copy the handle, but not the rep. If the handle is an ordinary pointer, this will not work, since we'll end up with two Strings pointing at the same rep. When one of the Strings is destroyed, the rep will be destroyed also, leaving the other String pointing to freed memory.

To avoid this, our String copy constructor will create a new rep:

```
String::String(const String& s)
: rep(new char[strlen(s.rep)+1]) {
    strcpy(rep,s.rep);
}
```

3.1.3   Assignment

Whenever the default copy constructor is wrong, the default assignment operator is probably wrong also, and for the same reasons. However, we not only have to copy the rep, we first have to delete the rep that represents the value being overwritten (see the discussion on page 32):

```
const String&
String::operator=(const String& s) {
    if (rep != s.rep) {
        delete [] rep;
        rep = new char[strlen(s.rep)+1];
        strcpy(rep,s.rep);
    }
    return *this;
}
```

With this implementation, we can have arrays of Strings, since every String object has the same size; the fact that their *values* have different sizes is hidden by the implementation:

```
main() {
    String t("C++");
    String s("ADD ONE TO COBOL");
    String array[10];
    array[0] = s;
    array[1] = t;
}
```

The memory that holds the characters is not part of the `String` object, so it does not affect `sizeof(String)`.

3.2   Avoiding copies with use counts

In our `String` class, we copied the rep every time we copied the `String`. We might be able to save some run time by avoiding the copy; we do this by making it possible for more than one handle to point at a rep. Copying a `String` can then be implemented by copying the handle instead of the rep. We avoid deleting the rep too soon by maintaining a *use count* in the rep, which is a count of the number of handles pointing at the rep. We delete the rep when the number of handles pointing at it becomes zero.

For our string class, we'll make a `String_rep` class that encapsulates the count and a pointer to the data:

```
class String {
private:
    class String_rep {
    public:
        int    use_count;
        char*  chars;
                String_rep(const char*);
                String_rep(const String_rep&);
                ~String_rep();
        void   increment();
        void   decrement();
        const String_rep& operator=(const String_rep&);
    };
```

```
        String_rep* rep;
    public:
        String(const char* = "");
        ~String();
        String(const String&);
        const String& operator=(const String&);
    };
```

The `String_rep` is a *nested* class; it is declared inside of the declaration of class `String`. Since it is declared in the private part of `String`, only member functions of `String` will have access to it.

A warning about nested classes: some C++ compilers may not support nested classes or may be buggy in this area. If your compiler has trouble with nested classes, you can get the same effect by making `String_rep` a nonnested class, with all members (including the constructor) private, and naming class `String` a friend:

```
    class String_rep {
    private:
        friend class String;
        int    use_count;
        char*  chars;
            String_rep(const char*);
            String_rep(const String_rep&);
            ~String_rep();
        void   increment();
        void   decrement();
        const String_rep& operator=(const String_rep&);
    };
```

This still prevents users from making `String_rep`s, but has the disadvantage of putting the name `String_rep` in the global name space (see Section 9.8).

3.2.1   Implementation of String_rep

The constructor of `String_rep` is straightforward: it gets the space for the characters, copies the characters into that space, and initializes the use count to zero. The destructor frees the space allocated by the constructor:

```
String::String_rep::String_rep(const char* cp)
: use_count(0),
  chars(new char[strlen(cp)+1]) {
    strcpy(chars,cp);
}

String::String_rep::~String_rep() {
    delete [] chars;
}
```

String_rep has two other functions that will be used by String. The increment() function will be called when a String begins using a rep; decrement() will be called when the String is done using the rep:

```
void
String::String_rep::increment() {
    ++use_count;
}

void
String::String_rep::decrement() {
    if (--use_count == 0)
        delete this;
}
```

Since these functions are small and will be called frequently, they are excellent candidates for inlining.

The decrement function will delete the String_rep when it is no longer being used by any Strings. Functions like decrement that contain

```
delete this;
```

must be used with care, since these *suicidal* member functions can destroy the object they are called on. For this to work, the object being deleted must be on the heap. This will be always be true for String_rep, since the String constructor will build every String_rep on the heap—even if the String is automatic or static. Suicidal member functions should also take care not to refer to any members of the object after it has been destroyed.

Although our String class does not copy any String_rep objects, it's still prudent to consider whether the default String_rep copy constructor and assignment would do the right thing. If they do not, and we take no action, a subsequent change to our library that copies or assigns a `String_rep` will introduce a bug (see Section 2.1.2). As it turns out, the defaults *are* wrong, since they would just copy the `chars` pointer. While we could get away with just making the copy constructor and assignment operators private, it will be instructive to actually implement them.

Both functions will copy the characters pointed at by the `chars` pointer. The `use_count` member is more interesting; it holds a count of the number of `Strings` pointing at the object. When an object contains a data member (like the use count) that contains information about the *object*, and not its *value*, the default copy constructor and assignment operator must usually be specially implemented to *not* copy that data member. The copy constructor should initialize that member to whatever value is right for a new object, and the assignment operator should not change that member at all:

```
String::String_rep::String_rep(
    const String::String_rep& orig)
: use_count(0),
  chars(new char[strlen(orig.chars)+1]) {
    strcpy(chars,orig.chars);
}

const String::String_rep&
String::String_rep::operator=(
    const String::String_rep& orig) {
    if (this != &orig) {
        delete [] chars;
        chars = new char[strlen(orig.chars)+1];
        strcpy(chars,orig.chars);
    }
    // use_count is unchanged
    return *this;
}
```

The `String_rep` copy constructor initializes `use_count` to zero, and the assignment operator does not change the use count.

3.2.2 String implementation

The `String` class must maintain the use counts in the `String_reps`. This will involve a call to `increment` whenever a `String` is created and a call to decrement whenever a String is destroyed:

```
String::String(const char* c)
: rep(new String_rep(c)) {
    rep->increment();
}

String::~String() {
    rep->decrement();
}

String::String(const String& s)
: rep(s.rep) {
    rep->increment();
}
```

Any operation that changes the value of String::rep must also update the counts:

```
const String&
String::operator=(const String& s) {
    if (rep != s.rep) {
        rep->decrement();
        rep = s.rep;
        rep->increment();
    }
    return *this;
}
```

Again, the assignment operator must be careful to check for the s = s case, since the call to decrement can destroy the rep.

Note that a String never explicitly deletes a String_rep, it just decrements the rep. When the count reaches zero, String_rep::decrement destroys the rep.

3.2.3   Copy on write

The fact that two or more Strings can share a rep is an implementation detail; any operation that changes the value of a String must make sure that any other Strings sharing the rep do not have their values changed. This is normally done by having every such operation allocate a new rep to hold the changed value (although this should be optimized away if the use count of the old rep is 1). For example, a member function that forced all characters in a String to be lower case might do it this way:

```
#include <ctype.h>
void
String::to_lower() {
    if (rep->use_count > 1) {
        String_rep* new_rep =
            new String_rep(rep->chars);
        rep->decrement();
        rep = new_rep;
        rep->increment();
    }
    assert(rep->use_count == 1);
    for (char* cp = rep->chars; *cp; ++cp)
        *cp = tolower(*cp);
}
```

This function ensures that its rep is not shared before it converts the characters to lower case.

3.2.4   A caveat

A use-counted class is more complicated than a non-use-counted equivalent, and all of this horsing around with use counts takes a significant amount of processing time. If the time spent copying values is small enough (either because the values are small and cheap to copy or they are not copied very often), changing the class to do use counting may make programs *slower*. Always do some performance measurements when making this kind of change to convince yourself that this optimization is not really a pessimization!

As an example, let's compare the performance of our use-counted String class with the original (non-use-counted) version. I used a test program that created 1000 empty Strings, assigned to each String from 0 to 3 times, and then destroyed it.

Since the benefit of use counting comes from not copying the characters in the String, we would expect the use-counted scheme to win when strings are large and their values are copied many times. That was the case on my machine. If the Strings were never assigned to, just created and destroyed, the use-counted scheme always lost: creating and destroying a use-counted string was around 80 percent slower than the non-use-counted version. If each string was copied once, the two versions were pretty close, with a slight edge to the non-use-counted version when the strings were under 25 characters long. If each string was copied two or more times, the use-counted version was always faster. So, in this case, use counts win for some programs—those that assign to the average `String` more than once after it is created—and lose for others.

Code that manages use counts is also a good place for a careful code inspection. Bugs involving messed up use counts can be hard to find.

3.3   Avoiding recompilations: the Cheshire Cat

If the implementation of a class has been properly hidden, a change to that implementation should not break existing user code, but it will often force those users to recompile. For instance, a change to an inline function definition, a change to the size of an object, or a change to the structure of an object that is accessed by an inline function can make a recompilation necessary. Handles can be used to avoid these recompiles, so that a subsequent change to the implementation of the rep will make it necessary for users to relink but not recompile. There is some run time cost for this, however.

Carolan[1] describes a scheme (which he calls the "Cheshire Cat") in which two different header files are maintained. The public header, which you give to your users, merely declares that a rep class exists and that an object contains a handle to that rep. Here's a version of `String` that does not have use counts, but uses handles to reduce compile time dependencies:

```
// File String.h:
class String_rep;

class String {
private:
    String_rep* rep;
public:
    String(const char* = "");
    ~String();
    String(const String&);
    const String& operator=(const String&);
};
```

---

[1] Carolan, J., "Constructing bullet-proof classes," *Proceedings, C++ at Work '89* (SIGS Publications, 1989).

This file is almost pure interface—the only implementation detail it reveals is that a rep is being used. Functions that use any members of `String_rep` cannot be made inline in this file, since the declaration of `String_rep` is not provided.

A second, private, header is not distributed to your users. It contains the full declaration of the rep class:

```
// File String_priv.h:

#include "String.h"

class String_rep {
private:
    friend class String;
    int    use_count;
    char*  chars;
        String_rep(const char*);
        String_rep(const String_rep&);
        ~String_rep();
    void   increment();
    void   decrement();
    const String_rep& operator=(const String_rep&);
};
```

This private header file is used to compile the definitions of the members of both `String` and `String_rep`:

```
#include "String_priv.h"

String_rep::String_rep(const char* cp) {
// details omitted
}

String::String(const char* cp)
: rep(new String_rep(cp)) {
}
// etc.
```

Note that while the member functions of `String` cannot be made inline, the member functions of `String_rep` can, since all of the functions that refer to members of `String_rep` have access to the full definition of `String_rep`.

If class `String_rep` (the implementation) is changed, but class `String` (the interface) is not, your users will not have to recompile: they'll just have to relink. This is because the structure of their (**String**) objects has not changed, and no inline **String** member functions know about the structure of **String_rep**. The only code that knows about the structure of **String_rep** is code that the **String** implementor has already recompiled.

So, at the cost of an extra memory reference per operation, plus the requirement that none of the member functions that refer to the rep can be inline, we have ensured that future implementation changes (that do not change the interface) will require a relink, not a recompile.

Is it worth it? A judgment call has to be made on a case-by-case basis. The run time cost of the extra memory reference and the functions that could otherwise be inlined may be significant, especially if the functions are small and heavily used.

3.4   Using handles to hide the design

Someone who wishes to remain nameless[2] has said:

> A **friend** is someone who can touch your private parts.

That's true, but unless you explicitly prevent it, anyone can *look* at your private parts.

We say that C++ "hides" implementation details, by making it impossible to write *programs* that depend on the private parts of a class. But there's nothing to prevent *humans* from examining the parts of the implementation declared in the header files.

As a class provider, you may want to prevent your customers from even *reading* about your implementation. For instance, your class may be designed around a proprietary algorithm that you do not wish to share. If you use the "Cheshire cat" and do not deliver the source for the private header file, your users will be unable to learn anything about your implementation. Make sure that the binaries you deliver do not contain debugging information that describes the rep!

3.5   Multiple implementations

When an object's implementation uses handles, its constructor can choose from several different implementations when building the rep. For instance,

---

[2]But you'd recognize the name.

we might have two different implementations of the rep for `String`: one that was fast but worked only for short strings, and one that was slower but worked for strings of any length. The `String` constructor could then look at the length of the string it was building and choose the appropriate implementation.

This is done by deriving the implementation classes from a common base class.   For our `String` class, `String_rep` will be the common base class that specifies the operations to be supported by both implementations. These implementations are provided by the derived classes `Small_rep` and `Big_rep`. Each `String` object will contain a `String_rep*` handle that will point to either a `Small_rep` or a `Big_rep`. All access to the rep will be done by virtual function calls through the handle:

```
class String {
private:

    class String_rep {
    public:
      virtual String_rep* copy() const = 0;
      virtual ~String_rep() {}
      virtual char operator[](int) const = 0;
      // Other operations omitted...
    };

    class Small_rep : public String_rep {
    public:
      Small_rep(const char*);
      ~Small_rep();
      String_rep* copy() const;
      char operator[](int) const;
    };

    class Big_rep : public String_rep {
    public:
      Big_rep(const char*);
      ~Big_rep();
      String_rep* copy() const;
      char operator[](int) const;
    };

    String_rep* rep;
```

```
public:
    String(const char* = "");
    String(const String&);
    ~String();
    const String& operator=(const String&);
    char operator[](int) const;
    // Other operations omitted
};
```

The = 0 in the declaration of `String_rep::copy` and `String_rep::opera-tor[]` indicates that these are *pure virtual functions* which will be overridden in the derived classes. We'll talk more about pure virtual functions in Section 4.6.

`String_rep` has a virtual destructor but no constructor. The virtual destructor's only purpose is to force all of the destructors in the derived classes to be virtual; this ensures that a `delete` of a `String_rep*` will call the destructor in the derived class.

Each `String` object needs to be able to copy its rep (for example, to implement the copy constructor); since the `String` object will not know which kind of rep it is using, the copy must be done by a virtual function. `String_rep::copy()` will copy the rep it is called on and return a pointer to the copy.

The `operator[]` function is included as an example of a `String` operation that will be implemented by the rep.

3.5.1   The String class

Under this scheme, the only member of `String` that knows about the different reps is one of the constructors:

```
const int STRING_THRESHOLD = 4;
String::String(const char* cp) {
    if (strlen(cp) <= STRING_THRESHOLD)
        rep = new Small_rep(cp);
    else
        rep = new Big_rep(cp);
}
```

All of the other `String` member functions just call the `String_rep` member functions, without caring whether the `String` uses a `Small_rep` or a `Big_rep`:

```
char
String::operator[](int offset) const {
    return rep->operator[](offset);
}
```

Even the copy constructor does not know what it's copying:

```
String::String(const String& s)
: rep(s.rep->copy()) {
}
```

This manipulation of objects through pointers to a base class, without knowing the actual types of the objects, is what object-oriented programming is all about. We have defined a set of abstract operations on a `String_rep`, and all of the `String` members (except the one constructor) use these abstract operations only. This makes the `String` class itself more maintainable and extensible; for instance, if we wanted to add a new, third implementation of a string rep, the only member of `String` that we would have to touch would be `String::String(const char*)`. And, of course, the *user* of `String` has no idea that any of this is happening at all!

3.5.2   Operations that change the value

The use of multiple implementations gets much trickier if the value of the class can be changed in a way that makes it necessary for an existing object to change implementations. For instance, in our `String` class, suppose that `Small_rep` requires a string that is no more than four characters long, and further suppose that `String` has a member function that adds characters to an existing string. What happens when we add characters to a four character string?

One approach is to ensure that all of the versions of the rep work correctly with all possible values—they differ only in their performance characteristics. A string that is created with four characters and then grown to five may be slower than one created with five characters in the first place, but programs will still run correctly.

If this is not possible, an alternative is to have every operation that changes the value do so by building a new rep. The new rep is created by a function that chooses the appropriate implementation based on the new value:

```
String::String_rep*
String::build_rep(const char* cp) {
    if (strlen(cp) <= STRING_THRESHOLD)
        return new Small_rep(cp);
    else
        return new Big_rep(cp);
}

String::String(const char* cp)
: rep(build_rep(cp)) {
}

void
String::append(char ch) {
    /* Append a character to an existing String.
       First, build a char buffer with the new
       value: */

    const int len = length();
    char* newval = new char[len+2];
    for(int i = 0; i < len; ++i)
        newval[i] = rep->operator[](i);
    newval[len] = ch;
    newval[len+1] = '\0';

    // Now, throw away the old rep and build a new one
    delete rep;
    rep = build_rep(newval);
    delete [] newval;
}
```

append has to copy the data character by character—and getting each character takes a virtual function call. This is almost certainly too slow; how can we speed it up? We might try adding a function to **String_rep** that returns a pointer to the beginning of the characters, but this would force all implementations to store the data in contiguous memory. We'd like to avoid constraints on our implementations, so a better approach is to define a function dump that copies the character representation of the **String** into a caller-supplied character buffer:

```
class String_rep {
public:
// ...
    virtual void dump(char*) = 0;
};
```

This approach makes no assumptions about the implementation of the underlying rep; each rep class implements dump in the most efficient way for that implementation.

After implementing dump in our rep classes, we can rewrite append as:

```
void
String::append(char ch) {

    /* Append a character to an existing String.
       First, build a char buffer with the new
       value: */

    const int len = length();
    char* newval = new char[len+2];
    rep->dump(newval);
    newval[len] = ch;
    newval[len+1] = '\0';

    // Now, throw away the old rep and build a new one
    delete rep;
    rep = build_rep(newval);
    delete [] newval;
}
```

As we can see, the use of multiple implementations makes a class much more complicated; and, since every operation involves a virtual function call, there is also a run time penalty. However, multiple implementations allow the class designer to indulge in implementation-dependent optimizations, while keeping these optimizations totally hidden from the user.

3.6   Handles as objects

The examples in this chapter all use regular C++ pointers for the handles. It's possible in C++ to implement classes that act like pointers and to use these "smart pointers" to point at the reps. However, to properly implement smart pointers we need to use templates, so we'll postpone our discussion of this topic until after we introduce templates in Chapter 7.

3.7   Summary

Handles are a common C++ implementation technique. They allow the class developer the flexibility to have variable sized implementations, to reduce compile time dependencies, to make it impossible for others to infer implementation details of a class, and to have multiple implementations for the same abstract data type. All of these approaches have some cost at run time—at least, an extra memory reference for every operation—but that cost is often worth it.

3.8   In short

- Use handles to represent variable-sized values with constant-sized objects.

- The rep class should either be a nested class or a class with all members private and the "real" class a friend.

- Use counts can be used to avoid extra copies, but measure the performance impact to make sure it's really an improvement.

- Handles can be used to ensure that changes to the implementation (but not the interface) will require users to relink but not recompile. They can also be used to hide implementation details from prying eyes.

- Handles allow constructors to pick from a variety of implementations based on the constructor arguments.

- Handles need not be normal pointers; they can be "smart pointer" objects.

3.9   Questions

1. Explain the choice of the default argument to the `String` constructor. Why did we need a default at all?

2. What happens if the `String` constructor on page 64 is passed a null pointer? Decide on a better way to handle this case, and reimplement the `String` class to support it.

3. Reimplement our `String` class so that it stores the length of the string in the rep, rather than terminating the string with a null byte. Does this change affect the interface? (Hint: Can some strings be represented in the new `String` class that cannot be represented in the old one?) How will this change affect the run time performance?

4. The assignment operator for our use-counted `String` class has to check for the `s = s` case; why doesn't the copy constructor have to worry about this case also?

5. Suppose we changed our implementation of use-counted `String`s so that a `String_rep` was created with a use count of 1 instead of 0. How does this affect performance and maintainability?

6. Why wasn't `String::to_lower` named `String::tolower` instead?

7. Reimplement the `String` assignment operator on page 70 so that it contains no branches or loops. Compare the performance and maintainability of the two versions.

8. Under what circumstances could the **assert** in `String::to_lower` (see page 71) fail?

9. Suppose, in the use-counted string class, we wanted a member function

```
class String {
public:
// ...
    char& operator[](int);
};
```

to allow us to do things like

```
#include <ctype.h>
#include <String.h>
main() {
    String s("hello world");
    s[0] = toupper(s[0]); //s == "Hello world"
    // ...
```

Implement this in use-counted strings.

10. For the multiple-implementations version of `String`, design and implement a rep class that handles only null strings, but handles them very efficiently. (Assume that no `String` operations other than assignment change the length of the `String`.)

11. `String_rep::dump` stores characters into a user-supplied character buffer. An alternative would be to have it **new** the memory for the characters and return a pointer to that memory. What are the trade-offs between these two approaches?

Chapter 4

Inheritance

Many discussions about inheritance start with an explanation of the language rules. While we need to understand the rules to use the feature, we should first make sure we understand where inheritance should be used in a design. Programs with inappropriate inheritance can be made to compile, but such programs will be hard to understand and maintain.

4.1   The *is-a* relationship

Inheritance should be used when a new class (the derived class) describes some set of objects that is a *subset* of the objects described by the base class. This relationship is the *is-a* relationship:

```
class Vehicle {
public:
    virtual double accelerate(double);
};

class Aircraft : public Vehicle {
public:
    virtual double accelerate(double);
};
```

Every object that is an `Aircraft` *is-a* `Vehicle`. (Note that the converse is not true; there can be `Vehicles` that are not `Aircraft`.) Every operation that can be applied to a `Vehicle` should also make sense when applied to an `Aircraft`. (That is, the member functions of the base class can be called on objects of the derived class.) The derived class can change the *implementation* of a member function by overriding it in the derived class, but the conceptual operation should still make sense in the derived class. Every vehicle can be accelerated: a bicycle uses a different implementation of that operation than a train, but the conceptual operation is the same.

4.1.1 Inheritance vs. Composition

Inheritance should not be used when the base class is a component of the object described by the derived class:

```
class Wing {
public:
    double length() const;
};

class Airplane : public Wing { // Bad inheritance
// details omitted
};
```

An `Airplane` is not a special kind of `Wing` that happens to have a fuselage attached to it; rather, an `Airplane` is an object composed of other objects, including a `Wing`. (An `Airplane` is not a `Wing`, it *has-a* `Wing`.)

This inappropriate use of inheritance allows users to apply `Wing` operations to an `Airplane`:

```
Airplane a;
double l = a.length();
```

The call to `a.length()` will return the length of the `Wing`, not the length of the `Airplane`. That is not to say that the code cannot be made to work; but it is confusing: why is the wing treated differently from the engine or propeller? How can we have a biplane—a plane with two wings?

When an object is composed of other objects, the right approach is to make those other objects members, not base classes:

```
class Airplane {
  Wing w;
  Propeller p;
// etc.
};
```

This means that operations on the `Wing` part of an `Airplane` will have to explicitly mention the `Wing` member "`w`"; but this makes the relationship between `Airplane` and `Wing` clearer: it is *has-a*, not *is-a*.

4.1.2 Removing operations in the derived class

Every operation in the more general base class should apply to every object of a derived class. While the derived class can provide a new implementation of an operation by overriding a base class member function, the derived class should not attempt to *remove* an operation that is legal in the base class by making it private.

For instance, the (flawed) hierarchy that follows supports `Vehicles` with two different kinds of speed: the normal `speed()` relative to the ground, and the `airspeed()` relative to the air, which can be different from the `speed()` if there is a wind:

```
class Vehicle { // Bad design
public:
    double speed() const;
    double airspeed() const;
};

class Land_vehicle : public Vehicle {
private:
    // Land vehicles have no airspeed:
    double airspeed() const;
public:
    // details omitted
};
```

The redeclaration of `Land_vehicle::airspeed` as private is an attempt to make it impossible to call `airspeed` on a `Land_vehicle`:

```
class Car : public Land_vehicle {
// details omitted
};

Land_vehicle* vp = new Car;
double air = vp->airspeed(); /* Compile time error:
                               airspeed is private */
```

But the attempt is unsuccessful, since the forbidden member function can still be called through a `Vehicle*`:

```
Vehicle* vp = new Car;
double air = vp->airspeed(); // Legal
```

Attempts to restrict operations in the derived class usually indicate that the design of the hierarchy is wrong. To sort this out in our example, we need to decide whether it makes sense to talk about the `airspeed()` of a land vehicle. If we decide it does not, then the declaration of `airspeed()` should not occur in any class that is a base class of `Land_vehicle`. Instead, it should be moved to a point in the hierarchy where it always makes sense to ask about airspeed for objects of that class and *all* derived classes. For our example, we should create a new class `Air_vehicle` from which all vehicles that have airspeeds will be derived:

```
class Vehicle {
public:
    double speed() const;
};

class Land_vehicle : public Vehicle { /* ... */ };

class Air_vehicle : public Vehicle {
public:
    double airspeed() const;
    // details omitted
};
```

With this hierarchy, we cannot call `airspeed` on a `Land_vehicle`, even through a `Vehicle*`. (See question 1 at the end of this chapter for another way to fix the hierarchy.)

4.1.3   Private, protected, and public inheritance

A class specifies *two* interfaces to the outside world: one to the users (the public parts) and another to implementors of derived classes (the union of the public and protected parts). Inheritance works in the same way: if the *inheritance* is public, it is part of the interface to the users, and those users can write code that depends on the inheritance. If the inheritance is protected, it is only part of the interface to the implementors of derived classes; and if it is private, it is not part of the interface at all—only the class implementor (and `friends`) can use the inheritance.

Review: Public, protected, and private inheritance

There are three kinds of inheritance in C++: `public`, `protected`, and `private`. In all forms of inheritance, member functions of the derived class have access to public and protected members of the base class—but *not* to the private members. The three kinds of inheritance differ in what is visible to the *user* of the derived class (as opposed to the *implementor* of the derived class) and in the circumstances under which a user can implicitly convert a pointer to the derived class to a pointer to the base class.

The most common form of inheritance is *public* inheritance:

```
class Shape {
public:
    Color color();
};

class Circle : public Shape {
// details omitted
public:
    Circle(unsigned);
    unsigned radius () const;
};
```

When public inheritance is used, the public members of the base class are public in the derived class, and the protected members of the base class are protected in the derived class:

```
Circle c(5); // make a radius 5 circle
c.color();   // OK - color() is a public member of
             // a public base class
```

A pointer to a derived class can be implicitly converted to a pointer to a public base class:

```
Shape* sp = new Circle(5); // OK - Shape is a public
                           // base class
```

When *private* inheritance is used, the public and protected members of the base class are private in the derived class. They can be accessed by members and friends of the derived class, but not by users:

```
class String {
public:
    String(const char* = "");
    char operator[](int i) const; // i'th character
    int length() const;
};

class Telephone_number : private String {
public:
    Telephone_number(const char*);
    int uses_special_keys() const;
};
```

The members of `Telephone_number` can use the public and protected members of `String`:

```
#include <ctype.h> // for isdigit()
int
Telephone_number::uses_special_keys() const {
    for (int i = 0; i < length(); ++i)
        if (!isdigit((*this)[i]))
            return 1;
    return 0;
}
```

However, *users* of `Telephone_number` cannot call any members of `String`:

```
main() {
    Telephone_number tn("5551212");
    int len = tn.length(); // Compile time error:
                           // length is private
```

Users cannot implicitly convert a pointer to a derived class to a pointer to a private base class:

```
void f() {
    Telephone_number s("5551212");
    String* ptr = &s; // Compile time error: String is a
                      // private base class
}
```

With *protected* inheritance, the protected and public members of the base class are protected in the derived class. Derived classes can call member functions in the protected base class and can implicitly convert a pointer to a derived class to a pointer to a protected base class.

A public member of a private or protected base class can be made public in the derived class by using an *access declaration*:

```
class String {
public:
// ...
    int length() const;
};
```

```
class Telephone_number : private String {
public:
// ...
    String::length; // Access declaration
};
```

Users can now call `length` on a `Telephone_number`, just as if it had been declared with:

```
class Telephone_number : private String {
public:
// ...
    int length() { return String::length(); }
};
```

4.2   Public inheritance

Public inheritance is used when the inheritance is part of the interface. That is, the fact that an X *is-a* Y (X is derived from Y) is something that you are willing to tell your users about. Like any other part of an interface, you are (to some degree) promising never to change this part of the class! This is because users can write code that depends on the implicit conversion from a pointer or reference to `Derived` to a pointer or reference to `Base`:

```
void set_color(Shape&, Color);
Circle  c(1); // 1 cm circle
set_color(c,blue);
```

This code depends on the fact that a Circle *is-a* Shape, so the reference to the Circle c can be passed to any function that takes a `Shape&`. This means that you cannot change this class later by removing the inheritance, and expect existing code to work! That is an incompatible change to the interface—like taking away a public member function.

4.3   Private inheritance

Private inheritance is used when the inheritance is *not* part of the interface—it is an implementation detail. Users cannot write code that depends on the inheritance, which preserves your ability to change the implementation to no longer use that base class.

Private inheritance is used much less often than public inheritance, because composition (making the "base class" part a data member instead) is simpler and usually works as well. Rather than inheriting from the base class, a single object of that base class is made a member of the (former) derived class. There should be no run time or space penalty for doing this, and the resulting class will be easier to understand, since someone reading the code will not have to remember which member functions are inherited from the private base class.

For example, the `Telephone_number` class from the Review on page 88 should be reimplemented like this:

```
#include <ctype.h> // for isdigit()
class String { // As before -- no changes
public:
    String(const char* = "");
    char operator[](int i) const; // i'th character
    int length() const;
};

class Telephone_number {
private:
    String s;
public:
    Telephone_number(const char*);
    int uses_special_keys() const;
};

int
Telephone_number::uses_special_keys() const {
    for (int i = 0; i < s.length(); ++i)
        if (!isdigit(s[i]))
            return 1;
    return 0;

}
```

The only change to the code of the **Telephone** member functions is that
the implicit references to members of the base class **String** must now be
explicitly qualified with the name of the **String** member s. This change is
invisible to the users: their code will work as it did before. It is also unlikely
that the time or space used by their programs will change. Either way, the
object must contain one instance of the **String** part.

In most cases, a class without base classes will be simpler to understand
and extend than the equivalent class using private inheritance. Using composition also means that the later addition of a new base class will involve
single inheritance, not multiple inheritance. On many architectures, code
that uses multiple inheritance is measurably slower and larger than code
using single inheritance, and it is always much harder to understand.

The exception to this rule occurs when the derived class needs to override
a virtual function of the base class, but does not want the use of that base
class to be in the public interface. Private inheritance is the simplest way

to do this, and may be the only way to do it if the virtual function being overridden is the destructor.

For instance, suppose that we are using a C++ environment that supports garbage collection of objects derived from `Collectible`. Whenever `garbage_collect()` is called, collectible objects that cannot be reached using existing pointers will be deleted:

```
class Collectible {
public:
    Collectible();
    virtual ~Collectible() {}
};

void
garbage_collect() {
    Collectible* cp;
    while (cp = find_unreachable_object())
        delete cp;
}
```

Suppose also that we are designing a garbage collected class that represents nodes in a graph. While we probably cannot hide the fact that a node is garbage collected from our users, we *can* hide our choice of garbage collector. We do this by making `Collectible` a private base class:

```
class Node : private Collectible {
public:
    virtual ~Node();
    // details omitted
};
```

By overriding the virtual destructor, we ensure that the `delete cp;` in `garbage_collect` will call the `Node` destructor when a `Node` is collected. By using *private* inheritance, we preserve the option of changing the `Node` implementation to use some other garbage collection mechanism.

4.4　Protected inheritance

Protected inheritance is used when the inheritance is part of the interface to the derived classes, but is not part of the interface to the users. A protected base class is like a private base class that is known to all of the derived classes:

```
class String { /* ... */ };


class Telephone_number : protected String { /* ... */};


class Local_number : public Telephone_number { /* ... */ };
```

Member functions of class Local_number can access the public and protected members of their String parts.

I have never used protected inheritance, and I have never heard of it being used in a real project. All of the reasons for not using private inheritance apply to protected inheritance also—instead of having a protected base class, it is usually easier to have a protected member:

```
class String { /* ... */ };


class Telephone_number {
protected:
    String s;
    // details omitted
};


class Local_number : public Telephone_number { /* ... */ };
```

This rewrite makes the inheritance hierarchy a lot simpler. The performance is the same, and the member functions of Local_number can still access the String part of the object (although they must now do so by referring to s).

That is not to say that protected inheritance is never useful—if the members of the derived class need to override virtual functions in the (protected) base class, protected inheritance may be the way to go. But if you can use composition, you should: the use of obscure corners of the language (like protected inheritance) makes programs harder to understand.

4.5   Conformance to base class abstractions

A derived class can override a virtual member function of a base class by redeclaring it with the same name and arguments:

```
class Vehicle {
public:
    virtual void accelerate(double);
    double speed();
};

class Car : public Vehicle {
public:
    virtual void accelerate(double);
};

class Submarine : public Vehicle {
public:
    virtual void accelerate(double);
};
```

However, when using inheritance, there is a much stronger constraint on the `accelerate` members of `Car` and `Submarine` than just getting the types right. *The member function in the derived class should conform to the abstract model of the base class.* While the implementation may be different, any object of a class derived from `Vehicle` should "accelerate like a `Vehicle` accelerates"—whatever that means. This is a semantic constraint; it cannot be expressed in C++, so the C++ compiler cannot check for it.

For `Vehicle`, the abstract model for `accelerate` might specify that accelerating a vehicle changes its `speed` by the amount accelerated; that is,

$$accelerate(x) \implies (speed_{new} == speed_{old} + x)$$

Once this part of the abstraction has been documented, all derived classes should conform to it.

Why is this important? If all of the derived classes follow the abstract model, users can write code that depends on the model:

```
void
full_stop(Vehicle& v) {
    v.accelerate(-v.speed());
}
```

and have that code work for all `Vehicles`:

```
Submarine trident;
full_stop(trident);

Car volkswagen;
full_stop(volkswagen);
```

New `Vehicles` can be added later, and they will work correctly with code
that was implemented before they existed!

```
class Aircraft : public Vehicle {
public:
    virtual void accelerate(double);
};

// ...
    Aircraft boeing_747;
    full_stop(boeing_747); //Hope we're on the ground!
```

We have implemented a function that, by making calls to a set of abstract
operations (the virtual member functions), works with *any* class that derives
from **Vehicle** and correctly implements those abstract operations, without
our function knowing anything else about those objects. This is one of the
main benefits of object-oriented design.

If the relationship between **speed** and **accelerate** is not clearly documented and understood by the developers, someone will probably implement
a derived class that does not follow the abstract model. For instance,

```
class Hot_rod : public Car {
public:
    virtual void accelerate(double);
};

void
Hot_rod::accelerate(double delta) {
    //Hot_rods accelerate quickly!
    Car::accelerate(2*delta);
}
```

The author of `Hot_rod` has misunderstood how the `accelerate` member
function is supposed to behave. Therefore, `Hot_rod` does not conform to the
abstract model of `Vehicle`.

Consider what happens when we call `full_stop` on a `Hot_rod` that is moving at 100 km per hour. The `full_stop` function will call

```
v.accelerate(-v.speed());
```

which in this case will cause a call to

```
Hot_rod::accelerate(-100);
```

which will in turn call

```
Car::accelerate(-200);
```

After the call to `full_stop`, our `Hot_rod` will be going 100 km per hour in reverse! That is probably not what the programmer had in mind. Even though the code met the type constraints imposed by the language—it compiled cleanly—it did not do the right thing, because `Hot_rod` does not conform to the abstract model of a `Vehicle`.

4.6   Pure virtual functions

Our original `Vehicle` class included the declaration of an `accelerate` member function. We declared it in that class because `accelerate` is an operation that is conceptually valid for all vehicles. We anticipate that each derived class will override the base class version of the function.

How should we implement `Vehicle::accelerate`? We never expect to create a `Vehicle` object. Instead, `Vehicle` is a base class that describes concepts that are common to a *set* of derived classes. `Vehicle` is just intended to be used as a base class, and every derived class will override `accelerate`. So we do not expect anyone to ever call `Vehicle::accelerate`. One approach would be to provide a version that prints an error message if it is called:

```
void
Vehicle::accelerate(double) {
    cerr << "Vehicle::accelerate called?\n";
    abort();
}
```

but this approach only detects a failure to override `accelerate` at run time. A better approach is to use a C++ feature that lets us detect it at compile time—by making `Vehicle::accelerate` a *pure virtual function*.

Review: Pure virtual functions and abstract base classes

A virtual member function that is declared with "= 0" after the argument list:

```
class C {
    virtual void f() = 0;
};
```

is a *pure virtual function*. No definition of the pure virtual function C::f() need be provided. Any class that declares or inherits a pure virtual function is an *abstract* base class. An attempt to create an object of an abstract base class will cause a compile time error.

If a class derived from C overrides C::f, that class will be a concrete (nonabstract) class:

```
class D : public C {
    void f();
};
```

An abstract base class is used to declare an *interface* without declaring a full set of implementations for that interface. That interface specifies the abstract operations supported by all objects derived from that class; it is up to the derived classes to supply implementations for those abstract operations. For example,

```
class Vehicle {
public:
    virtual double accelerate(double) = 0;
    virtual double speed() = 0;
};
```

Since Vehicle is abstract, an attempt to create a Vehicle object is a compile time error:

```
Vehicle v; // Compile time error:
           // ``Vehicle'' is abstract
```

To use `Vehicle`, we must derive from it:

```
class Car : public Vehicle {
public:
        virtual double accelerate(double);
        virtual double speed();
};

class Bicycle : public Vehicle {
public:
        virtual double accelerate(double);
        virtual double speed();
};
```

Since `Car` and `Bicycle` override all of the pure virtual functions in the base class, we can create objects of these two classes.

Even though there can be no `Vehicle` objects, we can still use pointers and references to `Vehicles`:

```
void
full-stop(Vehicle& v) {
    v.accelerate(-v.speed());
}
```

A derived class that inherits (does not override) a pure virtual function is also abstract:

```
class Land_vehicle : public Vehicle {
};

Land_vehicle v; // Compile time error:
                // Land_vehicle is abstract
```

By making `Vehicle` an abstract class, the compiler will generate a compile time error if anyone attempts to create a `Vehicle` object. We do not have to bother writing the stub functions for the base class member functions. For these reasons, the use of pure virtual functions and abstract base classes is recommended for classes like `Vehicle` that describe sets of derived classes.

A destructor should never be pure:

```
class Vehicle {
public:
    virtual ~Vehicle() = 0;  // Bad idea
    // details omitted
};
```

`Vehicle::~Vehicle` will be called by the destructors of any class derived from `Vehicle`. Since we must have a definition of this destructor (otherwise we will get loader errors), it makes no sense to declare it pure.

4.7   Inheritance details and traps

There are a few tricks in the way C++ handles inheritance; let's take a look at them:

4.7.1   Things that are not inherited

Whenever you use inheritance, it is important to remember the things that are not inherited from the base class:

- Constructors (including the copy constructor). If a copy constructor is not declared, a copy constructor that calls the copy constructors of the nonstatic data members and base classes will be created automatically.

- Destructor. If a destructor is not declared and any of the nonstatic data members or base classes has a destructor, a destructor that calls the destructors of the nonstatic data members and base classes will be created automatically. The destructor will be virtual if any of the base classes has a virtual destructor.

- Assignment operator. If an assignment operator is not declared, an assignment operator that calls the assignment operators of the nonstatic data members and base classes will be created automatically.

- Hidden member functions. If a member function in a base class is not
overridden in the derived class and a function with the same name but
different arguments is declared in the derived class, the function in the
base class is *hidden*. For example,

```
class Car {
public:
    // Other stuff omitted
    void steer(int degrees);
};

class Autopilot {
public:
    Autopilot();
};

class Smart_car : public Car {
public:
    // Other stuff omitted
    void steer(Autopilot&); // Hides Car::steer(int)
};
```

Our `Smart_car` can be steered by an autopilot, but we have hidden
the base class version of `Steer`:

```
Smart_car c;
c.steer(45); // Compile time error:
             // can't make an Autopilot from an int
```

If you do not want the function in the base class hidden, you should
redeclare it in the derived class:

```
class Smart_car : public Car {
public:
    // Other stuff omitted
    void steer(int i) { Car::steer(i); }
    void steer(Autopilot&);
};
```

Some C++ compilers will issue a warning when a function in a derived
class hides a function in the base class.

4.7.2 Specifying `virtual` in the derived class

When you override a virtual function (pure or not), you need not explicitly say `virtual`; the compiler will realize that the member function has the same name and argument types as a virtual function in the base class:

```
class Base {
public:
    virtual void f();
};


class Derived : public Base {
public:
    void f(); // same as ''virtual void f()''
};
```

But it is good practice to supply the `virtual` anyway, to make it obvious to anyone reading the code what is going on. The meaning of the program is the same either way.

4.7.3 Virtual functions called from constructors and destructors

Virtual functions work a little differently when called on an object from its constructor or destructor. When a constructor is constructing the base part of a derived class, the object being constructed is treated as if it were an object of the base class, not of the derived class. This means that a virtual function call will invoke the version of the function that is appropriate for the base class whose constructor is currently executing, *not* the derived class.

For example,

```
class Base {
public:
    Base();
      virtual void debug_print()
          { cout << "Base::Base();\n"; }
};
```

```
class Derived : public Base {
public:
    Derived();
     virtual void debug_print()
         { cout << "Derived::Derived();\n"; }
};

Base::Base() {
    debug_print();
}

main() {
    Base b;
    Derived d;
}
```

This program prints

```
Base::Base();
Base::Base();
```

The call to `debug_print` in the `Base` constructor will always call `Base::debug_print()`, even if it is building the `Base` part of a `Derived`.

This puzzling behavior happens because the base class parts of an object are constructed before its data members. When the `Base` part of a `Derived` is being constructed, none of the `Derived` data members have been constructed yet. It therefore would not make sense to call the `Derived` version of a virtual function, since that version would probably try to access the uninitialized `Derived` data members. (To look at it another way, when the `Base` constructor is called, the object really is not a `Derived` yet; so `Derived` member functions should not be called.)

The same logic applies to virtual function calls in destructors:

```
Base::~Base() {
    debug_print();
}
```

This constructor always calls `Base::debug_print`, even if we are destroying the `Base` part of a `Derived`. By the time the `Base` destructor has been called, the `Derived` data members have already been destroyed, so calling the `Derived` version of `debug_print()` would not make sense.

Remember that this special behavior happens only when a virtual function is called on an object being constructed or destroyed. A virtual function call on some *other* object works normally, even if the call happens to be in a constructor or destructor:

```
Base::Base() {
    debug_print(); // Calls Base::debug_print()
    Base* bp = new Derived;
    bp->debug_print(); // Calls Derived::debug_print()
}
```

4.8   In short

- Inheritance is the *is-a* relationship: the objects implemented by the derived class should represent a subset of the objects implemented by the base class.

- Use public inheritance when the inheritance is part of the interface. Use private or protected inheritance only if the inheritance is a hidden implementation detail.

- Most uses of private inheritance should use composition instead; the exception is when the derived class needs to override a virtual function in the (private) base class.

- An overridden virtual function in a derived class should conform to the abstract model of the base class.

- Constructors, destructors, and assignment are not inherited.

4.9   Questions

1. Suppose, in our `Vehicle` hierarchy, we wished to define the `airspeed` of a land vehicle as a synonym for its `speed`. What does this do to the `Vehicle` hierarchy? Is this change likely to make these classes easier or harder to use?

2. How could you arrange for the `Vehicle` class to confirm that every implementation of `accelerate` in a derived class conformed to the abstract model? (Hint: you might arrange for the derived classes to

override some other function instead of `accelerate`.) What run time impact would this have?

3. A pure virtual function can be (but need not be) defined; such a virtual function can only be called directly, using the :: specifier:

```
Car c;
c.Vehicle::accelerate(20);
```

How might you use this feature? Is there a better alternative that does not use an obscure language feature?

Chapter 5

Multiple Inheritance

C++ supports multiple inheritance; a class can have two or more base classes. In this chapter, we will see how some designs can use multiple inheritance to model the public *is-a* relationships between objects. This is not the only way to use multiple inheritance, but it is the easiest way for programmers to understand and use, since it is a natural extension of the use of single inheritance to model the *is-a* relationship. We will concentrate on understanding what kinds of designs lend themselves to this use of multiple inheritance; most of the language nits will be left to the Reviews.

As an example, we will design a collection of objects that represent parts of C++ programs. For instance, one kind of object might describe classes, another might describe pointer types, and another might describe functions. These objects might be used in a C++ compiler or other tool.

5.1 Multiple inheritance as set intersection

A public base class encapsulates concepts that are common to some set of derived classes; we call this set of classes the *derived set* of the base class. For instance, a compiler writer designing objects that represent parts of C++ programs might have a base class `Type` that encapsulates concepts common to all C++ types. The derived set of `Type` includes the classes that implement the various C++ types, such as built-ins, pointers, and references.

We can look at this in two ways. Fig. 5.1 shows a typical inheritance tree, with the base class `Type` at the top, and the derived classes below it. (Some actual C++ types have been omitted to keep the diagrams from getting cluttered.)

Review: Multiple inheritance

A class can have more than one base class; each base class can be public, private, or protected:

```
class Derived : public Base1,
    protected Base2,
    private Base3 {
};
```

In this example, `Base1` is a public base class of `Derived`; the public and protected members of `Base1` are also public and protected in `Derived`, and a `Derived*` can be implicitly cast to a `Base1*`. `Base2` is a protected base class of `Derived`; the public and protected members of `Base2` are protected in `Derived`. `Base3` is a private base class of `Derived`: all of the public and protected members of `Base3` are private in `Derived`.

If two or more base classes have a member with the same name, and the derived class has no member with that name, an unqualified reference to that name is ambiguous:

```
class Telephone {
public:
    void reset();
};

class Computer {
public:
    void reset();
};

class Smart_telephone
: public Telephone, public Computer {
};
```

```
main() {
    Smart_telephone t;
    t.reset(); //Compile time error: ambiguous
}
```

In the hierarchy, an attempt to call `reset()` on a `Smart_telephone` is ambiguous, since each base class defines its own version of `reset()`. The ambiguity can be resolved by specifying the base class name at the point of call:

```
Smart_telephone t;
t.Computer::reset(); //OK
```

A more common way to resolve the ambiguity is to define a member function in the derived class that does the right thing:

```
class Smart_telephone
: public Telephone, public Computer {
public:
    void reset();
};

void
Smart_telephone::reset() {
    Computer::reset();
    Telephone::reset();
}

main() {
    Smart_telephone t;
    t.reset(); //OK
}
```

`Smart_telephone::reset()` hides the versions of `reset` declared in the base classes, so a call of `reset` on a `Smart_telephone` is no longer ambiguous.

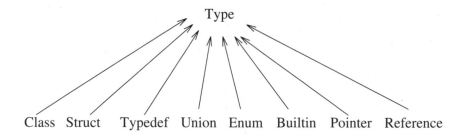

Figure 5.1: Inheritance tree for types

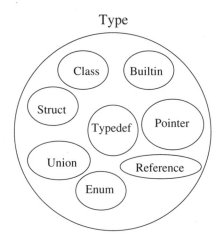

Figure 5.2: Types : Venn diagram

Fig. 5.2 is a different view of the same hierarchy.   This is a Venn diagram
of the universe of objects; the picture shows (for example) that every object
that is a `Class` is also a `Type`, since the `Class`es are a subset of the `Type`s.
The sizes and shapes of the regions are not significant.

Suppose further that we wish to have another base class for things in C++
that must be declared before they are used; such a class might encapsulate
concepts involved in matching names to declarations. Things that must
be declared before they are used include functions, data, typedefs, classes,
structs, unions, and enums; Fig. 5.3 is the Venn diagram for this derived set.

Declared

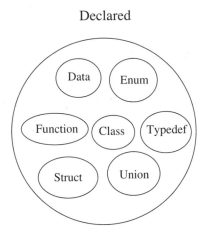

Figure 5.3: Declared things : Venn diagram

Now consider what happens when we attempt to use both `Type` and `Declared` in the same hierarchy. As we see in Fig. 5.4, the derived sets of `Type` and `Declared` intersect.

Neither `Type` nor `Declared` can be a base class of the other, since there are `Type`s that are not `Declared`s (built-ins, pointers, and references), and there are `Declared`s that are not `Type`s (functions and data). However, there are objects that are both `Type`s and `Declared`s; namely, `Class`, `Struct`, `Typedef`, `Union`, and `Enum`. Multiple inheritance is the natural way to model this. A `Class` is-a `Type` and also is-a `Declared`, so it has both of them as base classes:

```
class Class : public Type, public Declared {
// ... details omitted
};
```

A `Class` is now an object that supports all of the `Type` operations, and all of the `Declared` operations also.

If we do this with all of the declared types, we get the hierarchy of Fig. 5.5. This hierarchy has the is-a relationships right, but it is pretty unwieldy. We can simplify the picture—and our design—by creating a new class, `Declared_type`, that represents all classes that are both `Declared`s

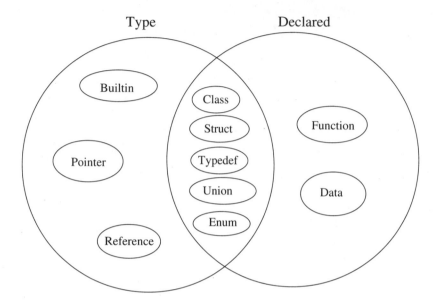

Figure 5.4: Intersection of `Type` and `Declared` : Venn diagram

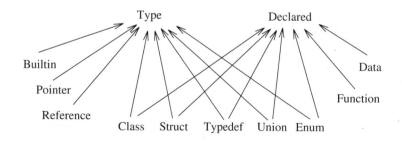

Figure 5.5: Multiple inheritance: first try

and Types:

```
class Declared_type : public Type, public Declared {
// details omitted
};

class Class : public Declared_type {
// ...
};

class Struct : public Declared_type {
// ...
};

// and so on
```

This gives us the inheritance hierarchy of Fig. 5.6.

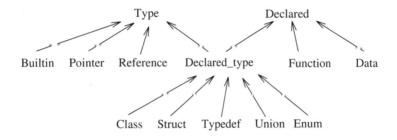

Figure 5.6: Revised inheritance tree

This hierarchy has a much simpler structure and is more maintainable, since it has only one class with two or more direct base classes. For instance, if **Type** and **Declared** have members with the same name, and that causes an ambiguity, we have to change only one class (**Declared_type**) to deal with it.

5.1.1 When *not* to use multiple inheritance

Multiple inheritance describes the intersection, not the union, of sets of objects. Whenever you say

```
class D : public B1, public B2 {
```

you are making an assertion that the set of things that are B1s and the set of things that are B2s have a nonempty intersection, and that all Ds are in that intersection. You can call all of the B1 public member functions *and* all of the B2 public functions on every D; so every D is both a B1 and a B2.

If B1 and B2 do not intersect, you should not be using multiple inheritance. In particular, it is *not* the case that "a D is either a B1 or a B2." A D is both a B1 and a B2.

5.2   Virtual base classes

When using multiple inheritance to model the *is-a* relationship, virtual base classes should be used when a derived class would otherwise contain two or more copies of the same base class. It makes no sense for the *is-a* relationship to hold more than once for two classes; either an X *is-a* Y or it is not. It makes no sense to say that an X *is-a* Y twice.

Let's look at how a change to our design might lead us to introduce virtual base classes. Suppose that some functionality is common across *all* of the objects that represent parts of a C++ program; we would like all such objects to be derived from a common base class (say, Program_part). The Venn diagram in Fig. 5.8 shows this: every object that is a Type or a Declared is also a Program_part.

How can we model this in our hierarchy? We might try making Program_part a regular base class of both Type and Declared:

```
class Type : public Program_part {
// details omitted
};
```

```
class Declared : public Program_part {
// details omitted
};
```

but this will not work, because each Declared_type will have *two* Program_parts in it. Program_part must therefore be a virtual base class:

Review: Virtual base classes

Consider this code:

```
class A{
public:
    int i;
};

class B : public A{};
class C : public A{};
class D : public B, public C{};
```

Every B, and every C, has an A part; and every D has both a B and a C part. How many A parts are in a D?

With the code as written, there are two distinct A parts in a D. Any reference to an A part of a D must be qualified (otherwise it is ambiguous):

```
main() {
    D d;
    d.i; // Ambiguous
    d.A::i; //Ambiguous: which A?
    d.B::i; //OK - the i in B's A part
    d.C::i; //OK - the i in C's A part
};
```

For many designs, having two A parts is not the right thing; instead, the two base classes B and C should share the same A part. This is done by making A a *virtual* base class:

```
class A{};

class B : public virtual A{};
class C : public virtual A{};
class D : public B, public C{};
```

All instances of a virtual base class in an object are shared; in this case, B and C share the same A part. If an object contains both virtual and nonvirtual versions of the same base class, only the virtual versions are shared.

A virtual base class is always constructed by the *most derived* class. In our example, the constructor for D is responsible for constructing the A part. The parts of the B and C constructors that initialize the base class A will not be executed in this case.

It is illegal to cast a pointer to a virtual base class to any derived class:

```
main() {
    D d;
    A* ap = &d; //OK
    D* dp = (D*) ap; //Compile time error
}
```

Dominance

When a hierarchy includes virtual base classes, the rules for resolving potential ambiguities get more complicated. When two or more base classes have members with the same name, and that name is invoked on an object of the derived class, the compiler will choose one of those names if it *dominates* all of the others. A name D::x *dominates* a name B::x if B is any (direct or indirect) base class of D. For example,

```
class Base {
public:
    int x;
};

class D1 : public virtual Base {
public:
    double y;
    short z;
};
```

```
class D2 : public virtual Base {
public:
  long x;
  void* y;
  char* z;
};

class D12 : public D1, public D2 {
public:
  float z;
};
```

In this example, D12::z dominates D1::z, but D1::y does not dominate D2::y. In practice, the easiest way to figure this out is to draw a picture, as in Fig. 5.7. There are paths from D12::z to all the other zs, so D12::z dominates; but neither y dominates, since there is no path from either y to the other y.

If no potential name dominates all of the others, it is a compile time error:

```
D12 d12;

d12.x; // refers to D2::x, which dominates Base::x

d12.y; /* Compile time error:
          neither D1::y or D2::y dominates */

d12.z; /* refers to D12::z, which dominates D1::z
          and D2::z */

d12.D1::y; // Explicit qualification can be used
```

The dominance rules are not affected by the access (private, protected, or public) of the names being declared. There can be an ambiguity, even if the code in question can legally access only one of the names involved.

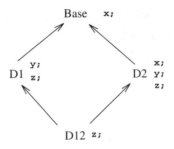

Figure 5.7: Dominance

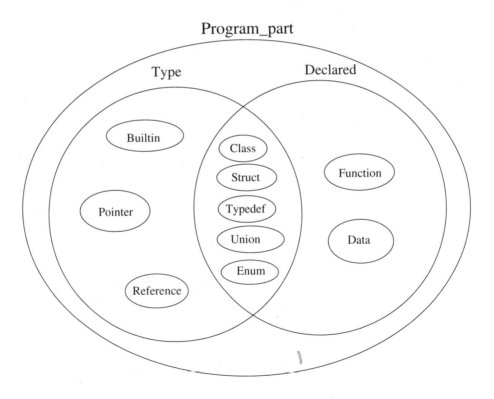

Figure 5.8: C++ program parts: Venn diagram

```
class Type : public virtual Program_part {
// details omitted
};

class Declared : public virtual Program_part {
// details omitted
};
```

Fig. 5.9 is the inheritance tree. The fact that there are two paths from

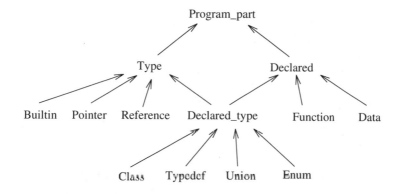

Figure 5.0: Inheritance tree, with virtual base class

`Declared_type` to `Program_part` is the indication that virtual bases should be used.

As we will see in this chapter and Chapter 6, virtual bases make things more complicated, so you should not add them unless they are needed. But for a design like ours, where two intersecting sets are themselves subsets of the same (third) set, virtual base classes provide the right model for the *is-a* relationships.

5.3   Some multiple inheritance details

In this section, we look at some details of multiple inheritance.

5.3.1   Name ambiguities

There can be an ambiguity if two or more base classes declare (or inherit) member functions with the same name. For instance, suppose that both

Types and Declareds have a function named make_String that returns a String representation of the object:

```
class Type {
public:
    String make_String() const;
// details omitted...
};

class Declared {
public:
    String make_String() const;
// details omitted...
};
```

Any call to make_String on a Declared_type is ambiguous.

Name ambiguities are often (but not always) a sign that the design is not quite right. In this case, we should ask ourselves whether the make_String operation applies only to Types and Declareds or whether it applies to all program parts. If it applies to all program parts, the declaration of make_String should be moved into class Program_part. If a single implementation will work for all Program_parts, we can remove the other declarations of make_String, and the ambiguity is resolved. If Type and Declared require different implementations of make_String or if make_String should not be a member of Program_part, we can repair the ambiguity by declaring and defining Declared_type::make_String, which will hide the base class versions of that function:

```
class Declared_type : public Type, public Declared {
public:
    String make_String() const;
};
```

This removes the ambiguity.

5.3.2   Initialization of base classes

The order in which the base classes are listed in a class declaration determines three things:

- The base class parts of a derived class will be constructed in the order in which they are listed. When building a Declared_type, the Type part will be constructed before the `Declared` part. (Virtual base classes are an exception; see below.)

Just as with member initialization (see page 28), the order in the class declaration, *not* in the definition of the constructor, is used.

- The base class parts of a derived class will be destroyed in the reverse of the order in which they were constructed.

- Some details of the storage layout depend on the order, but most programs should be unaffected.

5.3.3 Initialization of virtual base classes

If a virtual base class does not have a default (no-argument) constructor, it must be initialized by *every* derived class. We talk more about this in the next chapter.

5.3.4 Specifying access levels

When declaring a derived class, the access level (`public`, `private`, or `protected`) should be specified for every base class. If the access level is not specified, it defaults to private if the derived class is a class and public if it is a struct:

```
class Base1{};
class Base2{};

class Derived : public Base1, Base2 {
};
```

Even if *you* realize that `Base2` is a private base class, the next person to read your code probably will not. This is much clearer:

```
class Derived : public Base1, private Base2 {
};
```

5.4 In short

- Use multiple inheritance when the *is-a* relationship holds between a derived class and two (or more) base classes and neither of those base classes is a subset of the other.

- Use virtual base classes to avoid duplication of the base parts of an object.

- The base class parts are constructed in the order they appear in the class declaration, not the constructor definition.

- Explicitly state the protection of every base class.

5.5   Questions

1. Fig. 5.10 is a Venn diagram of three base classes A, B, and C. Write

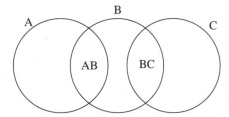

Figure 5.10: Venn diagram for three intersecting classes

declarations of the derived classes AB and BC that do not duplicate any base class parts.

2. Fig. 5.11 is a Venn diagram of three base classes A, B, and C. Write declarations of the derived classes AB, BC, AC, and ABC that do not duplicate any base class parts.

3. For a hierarchy that has a virtual base class, write an assignment operator that copies the virtual base part only once. Is the run time saving worth the extra complication? What other reasons might there be for copying the virtual base part only once?

4. Should operations on virtual base classes have side effects (other than changing the state of the object)? Hint: answer the previous question before you answer this one.

5. Do the dominance rules (see page 114) work for classes that use multiple inheritance but no virtual bases?

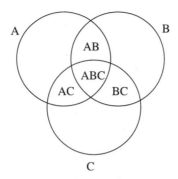

Figure 5.11: Venn diagram for three intersecting classes

6. Design a class hierarchy that reflects this relationship:

   "An X is either a Y or a Z"

   Assume that the derived sets of Y and Z are disjoint.

Chapter 6

Designing for Inheritance

A myth in the object-oriented design community goes something like this:

> If you use object-oriented technology, you can take any class someone else wrote, and, by using it as a base class, refine it to do a similar task.

Things often don't work out this way in practice.[1] If a class is not *designed for inheritance*—that is, designed with the intent that someone else would inherit from it later—and you attempt to use it as a base class, you will probably get stuck. To understand why such *unanticipated inheritance* does not work, we need to go back to the idea that a class presents two interfaces to the world: one to its users, and another to its derived classes.

6.1 The protected interface

According to the C++ language rules, a class's interface to its users includes its public members, and its interface to the derived classes includes the union of its protected and public members. But the lessons of Chapter 1 apply here: the *abstraction* provided by a class is more important than the particular type signatures and access permissions of its members. A class designed without a clearly understood and well documented abstract model will not be very useful.

A class that is not designed to be inherited from may present an excellent abstract model to its users, but the abstract model it presents to any derived

---

[1] Carroll, M., "Problems with Non-invasive Inheritance in C++," *Proceedings of the 1991 USENIX C++ Conference*, pp. 13–27.

classes is essentially random! The odds that a random interface will be useful are pretty small.

We should emphasize that we are talking about designing a class that *someone else* will use as a base class. Obviously, if you are the sole owner of all of the classes in an inheritance hierarchy, you can fix any of the problems we are about to discuss simply by fixing the appropriate base class. Worrying about unanticipated inheritance is less important in this case. The problems come when the user does not own the source for the base class that needs to be fixed.

Let's look at some of the ways in which unanticipated inheritance runs into trouble:

6.1.1   A member function in the base class is not virtual

Unanticipated inheritance often fails when the derived class needs to override a function that was not declared as virtual in the base class. For instance, if the author of the `Vehicle` class on page 83 had not made the `accelerate` member function virtual, any calls to `accelerate` through a `Vehicle*` would be statically bound (calling the `Vehicle` version).

Often the function that needs to be made virtual is the destructor. If the destructor of the base class is not virtual, a `delete` through a base class pointer will not call the right destructor if the pointer is pointing at an object of the derived class:

```
class Vehicle {
public:
    Vehicle();
    ~Vehicle(); //Oops, not virtual
};

class Land_vehicle : public Vehicle {
public:
    Land_vehicle();
    ~Land_vehicle();
};

class Tank : public Land_vehicle {
public:
    Tank();
    ~Tank();
};
```

```
main() {
    Vehicle* vp = new Tank(); //Calls Tank::Tank
    delete vp; // Calls Vehicle::~Vehicle
}
```

In this example, the `Tank` is constructed normally: the `Tank` constructor is called, which calls the `Land_vehicle` constructor, which calls the `Vehicle` constructor. However, when `vp` is `deleted`, the `Vehicle` destructor is statically bound—so the `Land_vehicle` destructor is not called.

If you expect anyone to derive from a class, make sure that the destructor for that class is virtual, even if that means creating an otherwise unneeded destructor.

6.1.2   A private member of the base class needs to be made protected

A derived class may need access to a private member of the base class. For example, consider a `String` class that uses `new` in its constructor to hold the character data:

```
class String {
private:
    char* rep;
public:
// details omitted ...
    String(const char* = "");
    ~String();
};

String::String(const char* cp)
:   rep(new char[strlen(cp)+1]) {
    strcpy(rep,cp);
}

// Copy constructor and assignment are similar

String::~String() {
    delete rep;
}
```

Now suppose that we want to make a kind of **String** that acts like any other **String**, except that it can be stored on a disk (it is *persistent*):

```
class Pers_string : public String {
// ...
```

Conceptually, there is no problem with this abstraction: a **Pers_string** *is-a* **String** that is persistent. However, when we take a look at the implementation for **String**, it is unclear how to implement **Pers_string**. The **String** constructor initializes the private **String::rep** member by calling **new**, which means that the characters for the **String** must be in (nonpersistent) memory. Since the **rep** is private, there is no way for us to override this.

6.1.3   Nonvirtual base class

Another problem happens when classes that were not designed for inheritance are combined using multiple inheritance:

```
class Vehicle {
/* ... */
};

class Land_vehicle : public Vehicle {
/* ... */
};

class Sea_vehicle : public Vehicle {
/* ... */
};
```

Suppose someone else wants to make an **Amphibious_vehicle** that is both a **Land_vehicle** and a **Sea_vehicle**:

```
class Amphib_vehicle :
    public Land_vehicle,
    public Sea_vehicle {
/* ... */
};
```

Of course, this does not work. Since **Vehicle** was not a virtual base class of **Land_vehicle** and **Sea_vehicle**, this **Amphib_vehicle** will have two

Vehicle parts: the `Vehicle` part of `Land_vehicle`, and the `Vehicle` part of `Sea_vehicle`. Only if the `Vehicle` had been a virtual base:

```
class Land_vehicle : public virtual Vehicle {
/* ... */
};
class Sea_vehicle : public virtual Vehicle {
/* ... */
};
```

would the subsequent multiple inheritance work.

6.1.4   Assumptions in the base class

The base class implementation may make other assumptions that are true for the base class but not for the derived class. For instance, the base class might assume that some information is unnecessary, or that some invariant (not part of the documented abstraction) holds.

6.2   Should you design for inheritance?

Does this mean that all classes should always be designed for inheritance? In particular, should we always make *every* member function and base class virtual? There are two issues to consider here: correctness and performance.

6.2.1   Correctness

Would making a member function virtual produce incorrect results? That is, given that a function is overridden in the derived class, would we ever want that function to call the base class version when called through a base class pointer?

```
class Base {
public:
    void foo();
};
class Derived : public Base {
public:
    void foo();
};
```

```
main() {
    Derived d;
    d.foo(); //Calls Derived::foo
    Base& b(d);
    b.foo(); //Calls Base::foo
}
```

It is very bad practice for a program to deliberately exploit this behavior. The whole idea of inheritance is that the *object*, not the caller, knows the implementation of a particular operation. A program that depends on different implementations being chosen based on how the operation was called is using the type system to control part of the implementation of the program—and in a very subtle way. If we assume that sensible programs are not depending on this behavior, making a function virtual should not cause anything to break.

How about virtual base classes? It is also the case that making a public base class virtual is probably not conceptually wrong. As we discussed in Chapter 5, the *is-a* relationship either holds or it does not; it makes no sense for it to hold twice. However, it is easy to construct a case where making a base class virtual will break an existing program! The problem is that constructors act differently when there is a virtual base class: *every virtual base class is constructed by the most derived class.*

Consider this case:

```
class Vehicle {
public:
    Vehicle(double x = 0.0, double y = 0.0); //Position
};

class Land_vehicle : public Vehicle {
public:
    Land_vehicle(double x = 0.0, double y = 0.0);
};

Land_vehicle::Land_vehicle(double x, double y)
  :  Vehicle(x,y) {
    // Other stuff omitted
}
```

```
class Tank : public Land_vehicle {
public:
    Tank(double x = 0.0, double y = 0.0);
};

Tank::Tank(double x, double y)
: Land_vehicle(x,y) {
    // other stuff omitted
}
```

This code as it stands is straightforward. The constructor for Tank passes the arguments that specify its starting position to the Land_vehicle constructor, which in turn passes them to the Vehicle constructor.

Now, change this example so that Vehicle is a virtual base class of Land_vehicle:

```
class Vehicle {
public:
    Vehicle(double x = 0.0, double y = 0.0); //Position
};

class Land_vehicle : public virtual Vehicle {
public:
    Land_vehicle(double x = 0.0, double y = 0.0);
};

Land_vehicle::Land_vehicle(double x, double y)
: Vehicle(x,y) {
    // Other stuff omitted
}

class Tank : public Land_vehicle {
public:
    Tank(double x = 0.0, double y = 0.0);
};

Tank::Tank(double x, double y)
: Land_vehicle(x,y) {
    // Other stuff omitted
}
```

Can you see the bug we introduced? Existing code that looks like this:

```
Tank t(1.0,2.0);
```

will, in fact, create a Tank with an initial position of (0.0,0.0)! This is because the initialization of the virtual base class Vehicle is the responsibility of the *most derived* class; in this case, Tank. Since the Tank constructor did not initialize Vehicle, the default Vehicle constructor was used. The initialization of Vehicle in Land_vehicle::Land_vehicle is not performed in this case, since Land_vehicle is not the most derived class.

The fix is to explicitly initialize all virtual base classes in every constructor:

```
Tank::Tank(double x, double y)
:  Land_vehicle(x,y),
   Vehicle(x,y) {
   // Other stuff omitted
}
```

As we can see, making a base class virtual is a major change: it imposes a requirement on *every* class that will be derived from it.

If the virtual base class has no constructor or has only a default (no-argument) constructor, there is no problem, since the default case will be the right one; this is usually the case if the base class is abstract and has no data. If there is no default constructor, users that forget to initialize the virtual base will get a compile time error. The case to be avoided is having a virtual base class with both a default constructor and a constructor that takes arguments. In this case, the designer of every derived class must decide whether to explicitly initialize each virtual base class, with the default constructor for the virtual base being silently called if he or she forgets.

6.2.2   Performance

What impact does designing for inheritance have on performance?

Making a function virtual imposes some cost. Each time the function is called, the object must be examined to determine which version of the virtual function is to be invoked. On most architectures, this costs a few extra instructions per call.

Making a function virtual also costs by disabling inline expansion. The compiler cannot expand a member function inline if the code to be executed is unknown at compile time.

Both of these considerations are important only for small functions, when the time for the function call overhead is a significant percentage of the execution time of the function. For larger functions, any change in the function call overhead will be swamped by the run time cost of the function itself. So, while it may be costly to make a small function virtual, making a large function virtual is unlikely to measurably affect the run time performance of the program; if you have any doubt at all, do not hesitate to make a medium or large function virtual.

As an experiment, I built an obvious `String` class that used an underlying `char*` representation. All of the member functions were small (one to five lines). I then built a program that sorted an array of ten `String`s. On three different platforms, I timed a version that had every member function statically bound and inline; a version that had every member function statically bound, but without using any inlines; a version that had every member function except the constructors dynamically bound (virtual); and a version that used virtual functions and a trivial derivation from a virtual base class. The optimizer was turned on in all cases. Table 6.1 has the results, with all times normalized to the time it took for the version that used inline functions.

Platform *Compiler*	Inline functions	No inline functions	Virtual functions	Virtual base class
SUN SparcStation 10 *USL C++ 3.0*	1	1.05	1.07	1.10
SGI 4D/380S *USL C++ 3.0*	1	1.06	1.08	1.13
IBM 386SX *Borland C++ 3.0*	1	1.10	1.13	1.21

Table 6.1: Normalized User Times to Sort an Array of `String`s

Design for inheritance can have a significant effect on programs that use the class heavily. (Remember that these numbers are for the entire program, not just the code that implemented the `String` class.) You should not pay this cost unless there is some benefit. On the other hand, the performance impact is not so great that you should warp your designs to avoid the use of virtual functions and/or virtual base classes. If the use of virtual bases and virtual functions makes your design cleaner, and the code easier to understand and maintain, it is probably worth it.

Notice that the difference between the "Inline functions" and "No inline functions" columns is always greater than the difference between the "No inline functions" and "Virtual functions" column. For these machines and compilers, the biggest cost of dynamic binding is not the run time cost of the dispatch, it is the fact that dynamically bound functions cannot in general be inlined.

Of course, all benchmarks must be taken with a large grain of salt. No doubt, if I had made certain changes to the way I wrote the code, I might have gotten somewhat different results. But the general idea that virtual functions and virtual base classes impose a moderate performance penalty seems to be true for most real programs.

6.2.3   Designing for inheritance has its costs

What we have discovered from all of this is that designing for inheritance has some significant costs to go along with the obvious benefits. Making functions virtual imposes a run time cost that varies widely, depending on the size of the function and the hardware architecture. Making members protected instead of private makes it difficult, or impossible, for you to change the implementation later without breaking any or all of your derived classes. A virtual base class adds a requirement to every constructor of every derived class. You should not pay these costs unless you are going to get something for it.

This decision is part of the interface to your class, and (like any other part of the interface) must be well understood, well documented, and not changed in incompatible ways.

6.3   Design for inheritance: some examples

Suppose you decide that your class will support inheritance by others. You should begin by understanding and documenting the abstraction presented to the derived classes. In the same way that every class should present a particular abstraction to its users, a class that supports inheritance should present a particular (possibly different) abstraction to its derived classes. The responsibilities (if any) of the derived class must be clearly documented and understood.

Do not assume that the interface to the derived class must make part of the implementation visible. Instead, you should strive, if possible, to hide your implementation from the derived class, for the same reasons that you hide your implementation from your users. In particular, while you may have protected *functions* that are part of the interface to derived classes, you should try to avoid protected *data*, for the same reasons that you should avoid public data. The existence of protected data makes that part of your implementation visible to all of the derived classes (see the discussion in Section 2.3). Performance considerations may make this necessary, but you should at least make the effort to hide protected data by providing protected access functions.

Remember that we are talking about the design of classes that will be inherited from by others. Protected data may be perfectly reasonable if you own all of the derived classes. But if you are designing your class to be inherited from by *others*, protected data should be avoided.

When designing for inheritance, every class should declare and define a virtual destructor.

Let's look at some different examples of design for inheritance.

6.3.1   Abstract base classes

The "purest" (pun intended) form of design-for-inheritance is an abstract base class. Abstract classes need not provide any functionality at all; they may merely specify an interface. The derived class(es) are responsible for implementing the abstraction.

For example, here is a base class that specifies a simple character string abstraction:

```
class Abstract_string {
public:
    // No constructor
    virtual       ~Abstract_string() {}
    virtual char  operator[](int) const = 0;
    virtual int   length() const = 0;
    virtual void  output(ostream&) const = 0;
    virtual void  dump(char*) = 0;
};
```

```
inline
ostream&
operator<<(ostream& o, const Abstract_string& as) {
    as.output(o);
    return o;
}
```

Since there is no implementation for this class, there need be no constructor. However, we declare and define a virtual destructor, to ensure that any `delete` of an `Abstract_string*` will call the destructor of the appropriate derived class. This is one case where having a destructor, but no constructor, makes perfect sense! `dump` will copy the characters of the string into a caller supplied buffer; we used a similar function in Section 3.5.2.

Note the definition of the output operator. It would have been nice to have made `operator<<` a virtual member function of `Abstract_string`, but we cannot even make it a member function of that class, since the `<<` output operator is invoked with an `ostream&` as its first (leftmost) operand. (If an overloaded operator is to be a member function, it must be a member of the class of its leftmost operand.) So, we define a pure virtual member function to do the output and then define a nonmember `operator<<` to call that member. This operator will work with any object of any class derived from `Abstract_string`.

Abstract base classes provide the greatest flexibility for the derived classes; but since they provide little or no implementation, they also place the biggest burden on those classes.

We might use `Abstract_string` like this:

```
class Unicode_string : public Abstract_string {
public:
    Unicode_string(const char*);
    // details omitted ...
};
```

```
class Upper_case_string : public Abstract_string {
public:
    Upper_case_string(const char*);
    // details omitted ...
};
```

```
int
count_blanks(const Abstract_string& s) {
    int len = s.length();
    int nblanks = 0;
    for(int i = 0; i < len; ++i)
        if(s[i] == ' ')
            ++nblanks;
    return nblanks;
}
```

The `count_blanks` function does all of its string operations via virtual function calls, so it works with both kinds of strings:

```
main() {
    Unicode_string s1("hello world");
    Upper_case_string s2("foo bar baz");
    int blanks = count_blanks(s1) + count_blanks(s2);
    // ...
}
```

An abstract base class can provide some functionality. For example, we can replace the pure virtual `output` function for abstract strings with a version that is implemented using calls to the other pure virtual member functions:

```
class Abstract_string {
public:
    virtual void  output(ostream&) const; //No longer pure
    // Other functions as before ...
};

void
Abstract_string::output(ostream& o) const {
    int len = length();
    char* chars = new char[len+1];
    dump(chars);
    chars[len] = '\0';
    o << chars;
    delete [] chars;
}
```

This should work for any derived class that provides sensible definitions of dump and `length`. `output` is still virtual; this lets the derived classes provide a faster implementation if they wish.

6.3.2   Classes that provide a service to the derived class

Another kind of design for inheritance is a base class that provides some service to derived classes. Consider a base class that manages use counts:

```
class Uc_object {
private:
    unsigned int count_d;
public:
    Uc_object() : count_d(0) {}
    Uc_object(const Uc_object&) : count_d(0) {}
    virtual ~Uc_object() {}
    void increment() { ++count_d; }
    void decrement() { --count_d; }
    unsigned int use_count() { return count_d; }
};
```

Note the definition of the copy constructor. The default `Uc_object` copy constructor would copy the use count; but the use count of a newly created object should be 0 (see page 69). We therefore define a copy constructor that ignores its argument and sets `count_d` to 0.

Since the argument to the copy constructor is ignored, we can omit its name in the constructor definition. This is legal in C++ and is good practice; it makes it explicit that the argument is ignored, and it may be necessary in order to silence "not used" warnings from your compiler.

Code can register its use of any object of a class derived from `Uc_object`[2]:

```
class Widget : public Uc_object {
// Details omitted
};
```

---

[2] We will see a better way to do this, using templates, in Chapter 7.

```
class Thing_with_widget {
private:
    Widget* widget;
public:
    Thing_with_widget(Widget* w);
    ~Thing_with_widget();
// other stuff omitted
};

Thing_with_widget::Thing_with_widget(Widget* w)
:   widget(w) {
    widget->increment();
}

Thing_with_widget::~Thing_with_widget() {
    widget->decrement();
}
```

Any user of a Widget can notify the Widget that it is being used; and the use count of any Widget can be examined to see if it is being used by any object. Note, by the way, that the implementation of Uc_object is not visible to Widget.

Uc_object is passive in the sense that it just responds to calls from the derived class. A base class can also be active, in the sense that it calls (virtual) functions defined by the derived class. A simple case of an active base class would be an enhancement of Uc_object to automatically destroy the object when the use count went to zero:

```
void
Uc_object::decrement() {
    if (--count_d == 0)
        delete this;
}
```

Since Uc_object has a virtual destructor, the delete this will call the destructor of the derived class.

Of course, this scheme works only if code that manipulates pointers to Uc_objects calls the increment and decrement functions at the right times. It also imposes the requirement that all Uc_objects must be created using new—since calling delete on an automatic or a global is a no-no!

Having a base class provide a service to the derived class is just one way in which one class can provide a service to another. Other ways include the following:

- One class is a member of another (*has-a*); for instance, if a `Car` has-a `Engine`, that `Engine` member is providing a service to the `Car`.

- One class can invoke a member function of another class (*uses-a*). An object that needs access to a particular employee record may call a member function of a (separate) `Directory` object.

A base class should provide a service (by being designed for inheritance) when that service *changes the nature of the entire object*. C++ provides mechanisms that allow a base class to affect the entire object:

- The base class can call virtual functions that are overridden by the derived class.

- The base class can declare `operator new` and `operator delete` member functions that will be used when objects of the derived class are newed and deleted.

- A pointer to the base class can often be "down cast" to a pointer to the derived class. (This does not work if the base class is virtual or exists twice in the object.)

It is harder for an object that is a data member to get at the other members of the class or to affect how the entire class is created or destroyed.

Here are some examples of services that might reasonably be provided by a base class:

- Make the object persistent;

- Issue a debug print when the object is created and destroyed;

- Maintain a use count for the object (our `Uc_object` class);

- Provide a clever memory allocation scheme (`operator new`) to be used when the object is `new`ed and `delete`d.

Note that all of these classes would enhance the object as a whole in some way. Here are some changes that do not affect the whole object and should not be implemented using base classes:

- A new class `Manager`, which is a kind of `Employee` that also has an associated list of subordinate `Employees` (make a derived class, adding a data member that is a list of `Employee*`s);

- A new class `Big_shot_manager`, which can approve expenses with a different limit for each instance (make a derived class, adding a data member that is the approval limit.)

If you are unsure, try using composition first. If that cannot possibly work, then consider using a base class. For example, it should be clear that making a class persistent by adding a new data member is wrong: you are not adding a new persistent part to the class, you are making the whole class persistent.

6.4   Summary

When you are designing for inheritance by others, apply the same fundamental principles of data abstraction that you use in any other class; just keep in mind that you have two audiences instead of one. Avoid making the implementation visible to the derived class. You should know, in advance, how others will be using your class, and design the interface to the derived classes accordingly.

6.5   In short

- Every class presents two interfaces: one to the users, another to the derived classes.

- For a class to be useful as a base class, both interfaces (and their associated abstract models) must be designed and documented.

- Design for inheritance involves run time penalties and more complex abstract models. It is a feature that belongs in some classes, but not in all classes.

- Any class that will be inherited from should have a virtual destructor.

- Virtual base classes are initialized by the most derived class.

- Avoid protected data.

- Making small, frequently called functions virtual can make programs run significantly slower.

- Do not hesitate to make medium or large member functions virtual—it is unlikely to measurably affect performance.

- Use base classes to provide a service that affects the whole object.

6.6   Questions

1. Under what circumstances should a smart compiler be able to use static binding for a virtual function call?

2. Here is an attempt to generate a debug print of every string as it is created:

```
Abstract_string::Abstract_string() { // Wrong
#ifndef NDEBUG
    cout << "New String: " << *this << "\n";
#endif
}
```

Why doesn't this work?

3. Does it ever make sense to declare an inline virtual function? Under what circumstances?

4. Under what circumstances might it be very costly to make a large function virtual? (Hint: must all large functions run for a long time?)

5. Is the fact that it takes extra work to design a class for inheritance a consequence of the C++ language rules? Would it be true if we were using a different object oriented programming language?

Chapter 7

Templates

Templates (also known as *parameterized types*) can be used to implement data structures and algorithms that are largely independent of the types of the objects they operate on. For instance, a `Stack` template might describe how to implement a stack of arbitrary objects; once that template has been defined, users can write code that uses `Stacks` of `Strings`, integers, and pointers. The compiler will figure out which kinds of `Stacks` have been used and automatically generate the implementations of those `Stack` classes.

Templates are a way to tell the compiler how to generate code at compile time; in this sense, a template is kind of like a macro. Templates have several advantages over macros:

- Template definitions look like class and function definitions; macros often need extra syntax to keep the preprocessor happy (such as backslashes at the ends of lines to allow multiline macros, and extra parentheses to avoid potential precedence problems).

- Templates are automatically instantiated; the compiler detects the use of a template and arranges for its code to be generated if it has not already done so. Users of macros must figure out which macros need to be expanded and must make sure that a macro is not expanded twice for the same arguments.

- Compilers generate better diagnostics for errors in templates. Errors in macros can be difficult to figure out, since most compilers will just identify the macro being invoked, not which part of the macro was in error.

Review: Templates

When you write a template, you are writing the specification for an infinite set of classes (for class templates) or functions (for template functions). Every template has one or more *template arguments*, which are usually placeholders for types.

When you use a class template, you specify the actual types for the type arguments inside angle brackets (< and >); the C++ compiler will automatically generate implementations of the template by substituting the actual types for the template argument types. (This is called *instantiating* the template.)

For example, if a `Stack` template takes a single type argument, then users can create and use objects of class `Stack<int>` (stack of integers), `Stack<char*>` (stack of character pointers), or `Stack<String>` (stack of Strings).

Note that templates take "type arguments" only at compile time; C++ currently has no concept of a run time "type variable."

A class template is declared like this:

```
template <class T>
class Stack {
// private members deleted
public:
    Stack();
    int empty();
    void push(const T&);
    T pop();
};
```

This `Stack` template has one argument T, which (because it was declared using `class`) is a type argument.

When *defining* template member functions, the `template` keyword and the type arguments must be repeated prior to each definition; and the template arguments (but not the `template` or `class` keywords) must also be supplied as part of the name of the function:

```
template<class T>
Stack<T>::Stack() {
  // details omitted
}

template<class T>
int
Stack<T>::empty() {
  // details omitted
}

template <class T>
void
Stack<T>::push(const T& arg) {
  // details omitted
}

template <class T>
T
Stack<T>::pop() {
  // details omitted
}
```

The template arguments are specified only once when defining a template constructor; we define Stack<T>::Stack, not Stack<T>::Stack<T>.

Even though the class keyword is used to indicate a type argument to a template, the actual type argument can be any type—it need not be a class:

```
Stack<char*> ptr_stack; //OK
```

All of these advantages accrue because templates are part of the language, while macros are not.

7.1   A `Pair` class template

Let's start by building a simple class template. In C++, only one object can be returned from a function. The designer of a function that needs to return two objects has two choices.

The function can "return" one or both of the objects by requiring the caller to pass a pointer or reference that the called function stores into, but this has some disadvantages:

- The caller must explicitly define the object being stored into. This is at the least a bother, and can be problematic if the object has a constructor but no default constructor.

- If the object has a constructor, "returning" it from a function usually involves creating the object using the default constructor. The called function then sets the value of the object using assignment. As we saw in Section 2.1.3, initializing an object with the default constructor and then assigning to it is usually slower than initializing it with the right value.

- The fact that a function stores through one of its reference arguments may not be obvious from the call.

- If the caller passes a reference to an object of a derived class, only the base class part of that object will be changed by the store. This can leave the object in an insane state.

The alternative is to have the function return a single class object that contains both of the return values. We will design a `Pair<L,R>` template that automates this second option, so that we can use `Pair`s of objects without having to explicitly declare and define each kind of `Pair`. For example,

```
Pair<String,int> find_highest_salary(const Database&);

void
print_highest_salary(Database& db) {
    Pair<String,int> rch = find_highest_salary(db);
    cout << rch.left() << " earns " << rch.right() << endl;
}
```

A Pair<L,R> is simply an object that contains an L and an R:

```
template <class L, class R>
class Pair {
private:
    L         left_d;
    R         right_d;
public:
    Pair(const L& l_arg, const R& r_arg)
    : left_d(l_arg), right_d(r_arg) {}
    L         left() const { return left_d; }
    void      left(const L& l_arg) { left_d = l_arg; }
    R         right() const { return right_d; }
    void      right(const R& r_arg) { right_d = r_arg; }
};
```

That is all there is to it. We provide a constructor to initialize the members, but there is no need for us to provide a destructor. If either L or R has a destructor, an appropriate destructor for Pair<L,R> will be automatically created by the compiler; otherwise Pair<L,R> will have no destructor. The default assignment and copy constructors will do the right thing, so there is no need to program them explicitly.

One could imagine a Triple<L,M,R> template; however, at some point it makes more sense to define a new class, rather than have a function that returns (for instance) a Quint<A,B,C,D,E>.

What about overloading templates? For example, we might imagine a Tuple template that would take any number of type arguments. Alas, class templates cannot be overloaded; a program can contain only one class template with a particular name:

```
template <class L, class R>
class Tuple { /* ... */ };
template <class L, class M, class R>
class Tuple { /* ... */ }; /* Compile time error:
                            Tuple redefined */
```

7.2   Some template details

Any relationship between two instantiations of a class template must be programmed explicitly. Pair<int,int> and Pair<double,double> are two distinct classes; neither is derived from the other, and neither is a friend of the other. In fact, there is no way to say that all instantiations of a given template are friends; you can say

```
friend class Stack<int>;
```

but not

```
friend template<class T> class Stack;
```

or anything to that effect.

You *can* arrange for all instantiations of a template to name a particular class as a friend:

```
template <class T>
class Stack {
friend class Stack_impl;
```

and you can arrange for all instantiations of a template to have a common base class:

```
template <class T>
class Stack : public Stack_base {
```

Only `Stack` is a class template here; `Stack_base` is a nontemplate class from which all `Stacks` are derived.

Template classes can be supplied as type arguments to other templates:

```
template <class T>
class List {
// ... details omitted
};

template <class T>
class Set {
// ... details omitted
};

List< Set<int> > list_of_int_sets;
```

This declares a list, each of whose elements is a `Set<int>`.

The use of the < and > to delimit the type arguments of a class template causes a syntax wart. In this example, we had to put a space between the two >s that ended the template names:

```
List< Set<int> > list_of_int_sets;   // OK
List< Set<int>> list_of_int_sets;   /* Syntax error:
                                       unexpected '>>' */
```

If the space between the >s is omitted, the compiler interprets the sequence
>> as a right shift operator.

7.3   Template instantiation

When the compiler detects that you have used a template with a particular
set of type arguments, it instantiates a version of the template with those
type arguments by making a copy of the definition of each required function
with the actual template arguments substituted for the formal template
arguments. This (temporary) copy is compiled to produce an object file
that is then passed to the linker.

For example, suppose that we use an existing List template to implement
a Stack template:

```
#include <List.h>

template <class T>
class Stack {
private:
    List<T> list;
public:
    Stack();
    ~Stack();
    void push(const T&);
    T pop();
};
```

The definitions of the template members use existing routines in the List
class. A push inserts an element at the head of the List, and a pop removes
the first element in the List:

```
template <class T>
void
Stack<T>::push(const T& elem) {
    list.insert_at_head(elem);
}
```

```
template <class T>
T
Stack<T>::pop() {
    return list.remove_from_head();
}
```

If a user now creates a `Stack<int>`, and calls `push` and `pop` on that stack, the compiler will create and compile instantiation files that look like this:

```
void
Stack<int>::push(const int& elem) {
    list.insert_at_head(elem);
}

int
Stack<int>::pop() {
    return list.remove_from_head();
}
```

When the implementation of a template uses other templates, the instantiation process can iterate. For example, `Stack<T>` uses `List<T>` as part of its implementation. When the compiler instantiates `Stack<int>`, it will discover (after compiling the `Stack<int>` member functions) that it now needs `List<int>`. `List<int>` might itself need other templates, and so on. The instantiation process will iterate until all of the required templates have been successfully instantiated—or until there is an *instantiation error*.

An instantiation error occurs when the instantiation file does not compile. This can be due to a bug in the class template, or it can be due to code in the template that attempts to do something that is not legal for a particular type argument (see Section 8.7).

7.3.1   Implementation details

Unfortunately, the current draft of the ISO/ANSI C++ standard does not specify how a compiler must implement template instantiation. This means that you must consult your compiler documentation to determine (for instance) exactly where the definitions of your templates member functions should reside.

Pay particular attention to how your compiler caches template instantiations. A large project can use over 100 template instantiations; it is far too expensive to recompile them at every link. Instead, a reasonable compiler will instantiate each template once and then save the resulting object files in a cache that is used by future compiles. Some mechanism should be provided for updating the cache if necessary (e.g., if the definition of the template or its arguments changes). Again, different compilers handle this in different ways, so you will have to consult the documentation for your particular compiler.

7.4   Smart pointers

In Chapter 3, we used handles in the implementations of objects; those handles were themselves implemented using ordinary C++ pointers. Handles can also be implemented as class objects; these handle objects act (conceptually) as pointers, but they provide functionality that does not exist in C++ pointers.

Before we discuss the added functionality, let's show how a class object can be designed to look and feel like a pointer. Such a "smart pointer" uses `operator >()` to allow users to write code that looks like it uses regular C++ pointers. An implicit conversion to a regular C++ pointer also comes in handy:

```
class String {
public:
    String(const char* = "");
    int length() const;
    // Details omitted
};


class String_ptr {
private:
    String* ptr;
public:
    String_ptr(String* s) : ptr(s) {}
    String* operator->() const { return ptr; }
    operator String*() const { return ptr; }
};
```

```
main() {
    String s("hello world");
    String_ptr sp = &s;
    int len = sp->length(); // (sp.operator->())->length()
    String* dumb_ptr = sp;  // (sp.operator String*())
}
```

Look carefully at the last two lines of `main`. The call to `sp->length()` is really a call to the overloaded `->` operator on the `sp` object. (Note that `sp` is an object, *not* a pointer.) It is the `String*` returned by `String_ptr::operator->()` whose `length()` is taken. On the next line, the initialization of a `String*` with a `String_ptr` implicitly invokes `String_ptr::operator String*()`.

In practice, many of these "smart pointers" are independent of the object they are pointing to. Such smart pointers should be implemented as templates:

```
template <class T>
class Ptr {
private:
    T* ptr;
public:
    Ptr(T* p) : ptr(p) {}
    T* operator->() const { return ptr; }
    operator T*() const { return ptr; }
};
```

Now that we have defined the template, we can use a `Ptr<String>` ("pointer to `String`") in our code:

```
main() {
    String s("hello world");
    Ptr<String> sp = &s;
    int len = sp->length(); // as before...
    String* dumb_ptr = sp; // as before...
}
```

All of the member functions of `Ptr` are inline, so this code is no slower than code that uses regular C++ pointers. Of course, a smart pointer that has extra functionality may be slower than a regular pointer; but that is due to the cost of the functionality, not to any run time overhead of wrapping that functionality in a smart pointer.

7.4.1   `operator->` and types that are not classes

Our `Ptr` template works fine for class objects, but if we attempt to instantiate a `Ptr<int>`, we will get a compile time error:

```
error:  operator ->() must return a pointer to class
object, a reference to class object, or a class object
```

The compiler is objecting to the declaration (in the instantiated template) of `Ptr<int>::operator->`, since its only use would be to access members of ints—which is impossible, since `int` is not a class. If you intend to support smart pointers to non class types, you will need to provide two kinds of smart pointers: one that declares `operator->`, and one that does not. We can use public inheritance here; an `NCPtr<T>` ("nonclass pointer") does not declare `operator->`, so T can be any type; the derived class `Ptr<T>` adds the declaration of `operator->`:

```
// pointer to any type:
template <class T>
class NCPtr {
private:
    T* ptr;
public:
    NCPtr(T* p) : ptr(p) {}
    operator T*() const { return ptr; }
};

// pointer to class object:
template <class T>
class Ptr : public NCPtr<T> {
public:
    Ptr(T* p) : NCPtr<T>(p) {}
    T* operator->() const { return (T*)(*this); }
};

main() {
    int i;
    NCPtr<int> ip = &i;
    String s;
    Ptr<String> sp = &s;
    int len = sp->length();
}
```

Note that we have rewritten `Ptr<T>::operator->` to use the public interface of `NCPtr`; this allows us to keep the data member `NCPtr<T>::ptr` private.

So far, our smart pointers are no smarter than regular pointers. Let's add some extra functionality to them.

7.4.2   A use-counted smart pointer template

In this section we implement a smart pointer template that emulates a kind of garbage collection—implemented with use counts. All use-counted objects will be derived from (nontemplate) class `Uc_object`. Such objects must always be allocated from the free store using **new**. Every use-counted object of class `T` may have any number of `Uc_ptr<T>` objects pointing to it at any time. When the number of `Uc_ptrs` pointing to an object changes from one to zero, the object will be deleted. (Note that the one-to-zero transition, not the existence of a zero use count, triggers the deletion. We take this approach because at the instant a use-counted object is created, it will have a zero use count, but cannot be deleted yet.)

We built the `Uc_object` base class in Chapter 6:

```
class Uc_object {
private:
    unsigned int count_d;
public:
    Uc_object() : count_d(0) {}
    Uc_object(const Uc_object&) : count_d(0) {}
    virtual ~Uc_object() {}
    void increment() { ++count_d; }
    void decrement() { if (--count_d == 0) delete this; }
    unsigned int use_count() { return count_d; }
};
```

The `increment` and `decrement` functions manage the use counts; `decrement` will destroy the object when the count reaches zero.

The `Uc_ptr` template will be implemented as a smart pointer that makes the appropriate calls to `increment` and `decrement` whenever the `Uc_ptr` is created, destroyed, or changes its value. Since the pointed-to object must have `Uc_object` as a base class, all `Uc_ptrs` must point at class objects, so we need not implement a version that does not declare `operator->`:

```
template <class T>
class Uc_ptr {
private:
    T* ptr;
public:
    Uc_ptr(T* = 0);
    Uc_ptr(const Uc_ptr<T>&);
    ~Uc_ptr();
    const Uc_ptr<T>& operator=(const Uc_ptr<T>&);
    operator T*() const { return ptr; }
    T* operator->() const { return ptr; }
};
```

In C and C++, an uninitialized automatic pointer has an undefined value. Our Uc_ptrs, on the other hand, will always be properly initialized (with a default value of zero). This is not only good practice, it is required to properly implement the assignment operator and copy constructor (as we will see later).

The two inline member functions provide the pointer functionality for Uc_ptrs. The rest of the member functions manage the use counts; these functions must take care to check for a zero `ptr`.

The constructors increment the use count:

```
template <class T>
Uc_ptr<T>::Uc_ptr(T* arg)
: ptr(arg) {
    if (ptr)
        ptr->increment();
}
```

```
template <class T>
Uc_ptr<T>::Uc_ptr(const Uc_ptr<T>& arg)
: ptr(arg.ptr) {
    if (ptr)
        ptr->increment();
}
```

and the destructor decrements the use count:

```
template <class T>
Uc_ptr<T>::~Uc_ptr() {
    if (ptr)
        ptr->decrement();
}
```

The assignment operator must check for aliasing:

```
template <class T>
const Uc_ptr<T>&
Uc_ptr<T>::operator=(const Uc_ptr<T>& arg) {
    if (ptr != arg.ptr) {
        if (ptr)
            ptr->decrement();
        if (ptr = arg.ptr)
            ptr->increment();
    }
    return *this;
}
```

We now see why we must not allow uninitialized automatic `Uc_ptrs` to contain random bits. The only useful thing to do with an object that contains random bits is to set its value using assignment; but that would cause a crash, since the `ptr` data member contains random bits, and `operator=` will call `ptr->decrement()` if `ptr` is nonzero. So the constructors must guarantee that every `Uc_ptr` is properly initialized.

Using the `Uc_ptrs`

We can now use `Uc_ptr` to re-implement our use-counted `String` class from Chapter 3. The rep class is a use-counted object:

```
class String_rep : public Uc_object {
private:
    friend class String;
    char*  data;
        String_rep(const char* cp);
        ~String_rep();
    // Other functions omitted...
};
```

```
String_rep::String_rep(const char* cp)
: data(new char[strlen(cp)+1]) {
    strcpy(data,cp);
}

String_rep::~String_rep() {
    delete [] data;
}
```

The `String` class will contain a use-counted pointer to the rep:

```
class String {
private:
    Uc_ptr<String_rep> rep;
public:
    String(const char* cp = "")
    : rep(new String_rep(cp)) {}
    // Other functions omitted...
};
```

Why is this better than the original version?

We no longer need to declare and define the `String` copy constructor and assignment operators, since the defaults do the right thing. Copying a `String` will copy the `rep` data member using the `Uc_ptr` copy constructor; and assigning to a `String` will assign to the `rep` data member using the `Uc_ptr` assignment operator. These operations will automatically update the use counts in the affected `String_rep`s.

We also need not provide a `String` destructor. The default destructor does the right thing: it destroys the `Uc_ptr` data member `rep`, which will cause the `String_rep` to be destroyed if and only if no more `String`s are using it.

Most importantly, the logic for maintaining use counts is now in a separate class that can be reused—or maintained—by someone else.

Use counting drawbacks

This scheme is not perfect. All use-counted objects must be derived from class `Uc_object` (but see question 5). The objects *must* be created using `new`; otherwise chaos will result when they are eventually `deleted`.

Objects that contain cycles of `Uc_ptrs` will never be deleted:

```
class Item {
private:
    Uc_ptr<Item> next;
public:
    Item() : next(0) {}
    void point_at(Item* i) { next = i; }
};

void
make_cycle() {
    Item* x = new Item;
    Item* y = new Item;
    x->point_at(y);
    y->point_at(x);
}
```

On return from `make_cycle`, the two `Items` are unreachable, but will not be cleaned up, as each has a `Uc_ptr` pointing at it.

Finally, if you have regular "dumb" C++ pointers to objects, these can be left dangling when the last "smart" pointer is destroyed.

Still, this pointer class has the advantage of making it possible to use a kind of garbage collection when you need it—and you only pay for it if you use it.

7.5   Expression arguments to templates

Most template arguments are types, but constant *expressions* can also be template arguments:

```
template <class T, int SIZE>
class Fixed_array {
// ...
};

Fixed_array<int,5> intray; //Array of 5 integers
```

Expression arguments are rarely used, since the same functionality can be provided by an expression argument to the constructor:

```
template <class T>
class Fixed_array {
public:
    Fixed_array(unsigned size);
// ...
};
```

Passing an expression to the constructor has these advantages over using it as a template argument:

- Nonconstant expressions can be passed as constructor arguments; expression template arguments must be constant expressions.

- When an expression is passed as a constructor argument, it is only mentioned once—when the object is initialized. When an expression is a template argument, it is mentioned every time the template type is referred to. A typedef can be used to get around this, but this requires inventing a new name for each instantiation of the template.

- All `Fixed_array<T>` objects are of the same type, so you can write a function that takes a pointer or reference to a `Fixed_array<int>` (for example) and have that function work with fixed-sized arrays of `int`s of any size. Getting that same functionality with `Fixed_array<T,int>` would require having all of the `Fixed_array<T,int>` classes derived from a common base class.

Expression arguments are usually used only when the performance of a small class is critical. The use of expression arguments can make some implementations faster, especially when those arguments are used in in-line functions. For instance, compare these two likely implementations of `Fixed_array`:

Size as template argument:

```
template <class T, unsigned SIZE>
class Fixed_array {
    T data[SIZE];
public:
    T& operator[](int off) { return data[off]; }
    unsigned size() { return SIZE; }
};
```

Size as constructor argument:

```
template <class T>
class Fixed_array {
    T* data;
    unsigned size_d;
public:
    Fixed_array(unsigned sz)
    : data(new T[sz]), size_d(sz) {}
    ~Fixed_array() { delete [] data; }
    T& operator[](unsigned off) { return data[off]; }
    unsigned size() { return size_d; }
};
```

Creation and destruction of a `Fixed_array<T,int>` will be faster, since it does not involve a call to **new**. Copying will also be faster. For instance, on a 16 MHz SparcStation, the time to construct a `Fixed_array<int>` of 100 elements is about 20 microseconds; the time to construct a `Fixed_array<int,100>` is essentially zero.

In practice, the performance speedup of a template expression argument usually is not worth the semantic restrictions (especially the constraint that the expression must be a compile time constant) and the extra typing.

7.6   Function templates

So far, we have talked about class templates; but functions can be templates also (see the Review on the next page). Unlike class templates, you do not specify the template arguments when calling a template function. Since the template type arguments must all be mentioned in the argument types, the overload mechanism can figure out the template type arguments from the actual arguments. For instance,

```
template <class T>
void
swap(T& a, T& b) {
    T temp(a);
    a = b;
    b = temp;
}
```

Review: Function templates

A *template function* is a template that specifies an infinite set of functions. For example, this template function swaps two values of the same type (note the use of nonconst references):

```
template <class T>
void
swap(T& a, T& b) {
    T temp(a);
    a = b;
    b = temp;
}
main() {
    int x = 5;
    int y = 7;
    swap(x,y); // now x == 7 and y == 5
}
```

Each type argument must be mentioned in the argument list of the template:

```
template <class T>
void foo(T*); // OK: T mentioned in argument list
template <class T>
void bar() { // Compile error: T not in argument list
```

Implicit conversions are not performed on template arguments:

```
long long1,long2;
int int1,int2;
main() {
    swap(long1,long2); // calls swap(long&,long&);
    swap(int1,int2); // calls swap(int&,int&);
    swap(long1,int2); // Compile error: no match for swap
```

The last call is an error because the swap template requires both of its arguments to be references to the same type.

```
main() {
    String s("Foo"), t("Bar");
    swap(s,t);
}
```

The compiler knows from the types of s and t that the call to swap is a call to swap(String&,String&).

7.6.1   An example template function

We can use our swap template function to build a sort template function:

```
template<class T>
void sort(T* v, int n) {
    for (int gap = n/2; gap > 0; gap /= 2)
        for (int i = gap; i < n; i++)
            for (int j = i - gap;
                    j >= 0 && v[j+gap] < v[j];
                    j -= gap)
                swap(v[j], v[j+gap]);
}

extern int int_ray[20];
extern String string_ray[10];

sort(int_ray,20); // Calls sort(int*,int);
sort(string_ray,10); // Calls sort(String*,int);
```

This sorts any array of objects for which operator< provides a total ordering relation.

7.6.2   Code duplication

It is easy to get a lot of code duplication with template functions. The rule that every template matches exactly means that there is, in general, a separate template function for every set of *static* types passed to the function; implicit conversions (like Derived* to Base*) do not happen.

We might try to avoid this code duplication by coalescing common code into nontemplate functions. That is harder than you might think. Classes have features (such as virtual functions, and implicit conversions from derived to base) that directly support coalescing of functionality; functions do not.

For example, let's take a look at how we would coalesce the common logic in our **sort** template. As a first step, we might attempt to restructure the function so that the T-specific logic is in as few places as possible. The T-specific code includes the array indexing (which depends on `sizeof(T)`), swap (which depends on T assignment), and the comparison of v[j] and v[j+gap] (which depends on T comparison using <):

```
template<class T>
void sort(T* v, int n) {
    for (int gap = n/2; gap > 0; gap /= 2)
        for (int i = gap; i < n; i++)
            for (int j = i - gap; j >= 0 ; j -= gap) {
                if (!(v[j+gap] < v[j])) //T specific
                    break;
                swap(v[j], v[j+gap]); //T specific
            }
}
```

We might then attempt to separate the function into a T-specific template and a T-independent nontemplate:

```
template <class T>
int
sort_hack(T& first, T& second) {
    if (!(second < first))
        return 1;
    swap(first,second);
    return 0;
}

void sort_common(void* v, int n) {
    for (int gap = n/2; gap > 0; gap /= 2)
        for (int i = gap; i < n; i++)
            for (int j = i - gap; j >= 0 ; j -= gap)
                sort_hack(?); // Oops, now what?
}
```

But we have a problem: there is no way for the general nontemplate function to call the template function. It cannot be passed in as an argument, because the type of the template function is different for each case. With objects, it is OK for the types to be different on different calls, as long as they are all derived from a common base class; there is no analogue for functions.

At this point we might be tempted to build some kind of private object to make this all work. A far better approach is to throw in the towel and accept the space overhead of multiple **sort** functions. The cost of the memory is almost certainly less than the cost of making a simple sorting operation into several pages of subtle code.

What does this all mean? Function templates should be used sparingly. Their best application is for small functions where the space overhead will be insignificant.

7.7   In short

- Templates are best used when the logic to manipulate objects is independent of the objects themselves.

- Any relationships between template instantiations must be programmed explicitly.

- When a class template is itself a template argument, add a space to avoid a syntax error:

      ```
      List< Set<int> >
      ```

  not

      ```
      List< Set<int>>
      ```

- The details of template instantiation differ from compiler to compiler.

- Smart pointer templates can be implemented using **operator T*** and (for pointers to class objects) **operator->**.

- Expression arguments to templates make the templates harder to use, but can be worth it for performance-critical classes.

- Keep template functions small.

7.8   Questions

1. What are the tradeoffs between using the `Pair` template to return two values from a function and creating a new class for that purpose? Consider ease of understanding, ease of use, space, and execution time.

2. Design and implement a "smart pointer" class that acts like a regular pointer, except that an attempt to dereference a zero pointer will cause a diagnostic to be printed followed by a call to `abort`.

3. What will happen if you use a `Uc_ptr<Foo>` when class `Foo` is not derived from `Uc_object`?

4. Our `Uc_ptr` class does not work for const objects. Does it make sense to provide use-counted pointers to const objects? If so, what operations should these pointers support?

5. Design a version of `Uc_ptr` that does not impose the requirement that the pointed-to class be derived from some other base class. Compare this version with the version implemented here: what are the tradeoffs?

6. Instead of a `swap` template function, we might try writing a (nontemplate) function that takes `void*` arguments that point at the memory to be swapped:

```
#include <memory.h>
void
swap(void* left, void* right, int length) {
    char* sav = new char[length];
    memcpy(sav, left, length);
    memcpy(left, right, length);
    memcpy(right, sav, length);
    delete [] sav;
}
```

Is this a good approach? If not, why not?

7. Why is `Fixed_array<T,int>` any better than an ordinary array?

8. Write a `sort` template function that, instead of using `<`, uses a user-supplied comparison function. Provide two versions: one that takes the comparison function as a template expression argument, and one that

takes it as a regular argument. Measure the speed differences. Does it make a difference if the comparison function is an inline function?

9. In the code on page 161, why did we write

```
if (!(v[j+gap] < v[j]))
```

instead of

```
if (v[j+gap] >= v[j])
```

10. Design and implement a "reversible pointer" smart pointer template. A reversible pointer should act just like a regular pointer, except that the pointed-at object can find out all of the reversible pointers that are currently pointing at it.

Chapter 8

Advanced Templates

In this chapter, we will see how templates can be used to build *container classes* that support fundamental data structures like lists and sets. We will then look at several ways to refine template designs and implementations.

8.1   Container classes using templates

A container class implements some data structure that "contains" other objects. Examples of containers might include arrays, lists, stacks, sets, bags, and dictionaries. Templates work especially well for containers, since the logic to manage a container is often largely independent of the contents.

Whenever you design or use a container, you should ask two questions:

- Is the container homogeneous or heterogeneous?

- Does it have reference semantics or value semantics?

8.1.1   Homogeneous or heterogeneous?

A container that contains objects of just one type is *homogeneous*. A container that contains objects of a variety of types is *heterogeneous*. In C++, a heterogeneous container will usually contain objects that are all derived from a common base class; this allows programs to iterate through the container, accessing each element through the base class member functions.

8.1.2   Reference or value semantics?

Does the container contain the objects or just references to them? A container that contains the objects is said to have *value semantics*. Containers with value semantics have the following behavior:

- No object lives in two or more containers (there is no sharing).

- An object is copied into a container; if you say

```
Container_with_value_semantics<Thing> container;
Thing t;
container.insert(t);
```

  a new **Thing** is created in the container (by calling the **Thing** copy constructor) with the same value as **t**. Subsequent changes to the **Thing** in the container will not affect **t**, and subsequent changes to **t** will not affect the **Thing** in the container.

- When the container is destroyed, the objects it contains will also be destroyed.

Containers with *reference semantics* do not copy values, they store *references* to objects. (We use the term *reference* in the abstract sense here; the implementation may use C++ references, pointers, or some other data structure.) When a container has reference semantics:

- An object can be "in" two or more containers, since each container just contains a reference to the object.

- Putting an object into a container does not involve copying the object.

- When the container is destroyed, the objects in the container are not destroyed.

- There is a problem when an object "in" a container is destroyed. Unless some mechanism exists to notify the container, the container will be left with a dangling reference.

8.1.3   Containers and pointers

Let's consider each combination of answers to our two questions:

Heterogeneous with value semantics

These containers are awkward in C++. A container with value semantics must copy the object into the container; but a heterogeneous container does not know the actual type of the object, so it cannot call the object's copy constructor.

Homogeneous with value semantics

Templates directly support this kind of container.

Reference semantics (homogeneous or heterogeneous)

While a container that supported reference semantics could be built, we can get the same behavior by using a (homogeneous with value semantics) container of handles. (These handles can be regular C++ pointers or smart pointer objects.) The use of pointers allows sharing. For a heterogeneous container, the pointers point to the common base class, allowing a pointer to any derived class to be inserted into the container. When a container of pointers is destroyed, the objects referenced by the pointers should not be destroyed (there might be sharing or the objects might be automatics or statics that cannot be explicitly destroyed)

For the container designer, therefore, a homogeneous container that supports value semantics should be the first choice. Templates support such containers directly; further, our users can get the behavior of reference semantics (e.g., sharing) by using containers of pointers. The one kind of container that is not directly supported—heterogeneous with value semantics—is hard to support no matter what you do.

8.2   Example: a `Block` class

Our first container will provide an abstraction that acts like a C++ array, with the extra feature that the size of the array can be changed at run time.[1] `Blocks` will be homogeneous, have value semantics, and contain objects of any copyable type. Run time performance will be the primary design goal:

---

[1]This class is modeled after the `Block` class of the USL Standard Components; the original version was designed by Andrew Koenig.

accessing an element of a `Block` should be as fast as accessing an element of an array. Here is the interface:

```
template <class T>
class Block {
// private details omitted
public:
    Block(int n_elem = 0);
    ~Block();
    void size(int); // Set number of elements
    int size();     // Get number of elements
    T& operator[](int);
};
```

The integer argument to the constructor specifies the original size of the `Block`. Each element will be initialized with the value of an otherwise uninitialized object of type `T`:

- if `T` is a class with a constructor, the default constructor will be called;

- if `T` has a constructor but no default constructor the template will not instantiate;

- if `T` has no constructor the initial value of an element will be undefined.

The two `size` functions set and get the number of elements in the `Block`. The overloaded `operator[]` makes a `Block<T>` look syntactically like an array of `T`:

```
// Calculate first 40 Fibonacci numbers:
Block<int> fib(40);
fib[0] = 1;
fib[1] = 1;
for (int i = 2; i < fib.size(); ++i)
  fib[i] = fib[i-1] + fib[i-2];
```

Since `operator[]` returns a nonconst reference, an invocation of `operator[]` can be on the lefthand side of an assignment (it is an *lvalue*).

We can calculate the next 40 Fibonacci numbers by growing the `Block`:

```
fib.size(80);
for (i = 40; i < fib.size(); ++i)
  fib[i] = fib[i-1] + fib[i-2];
```

Our `Block` template will guarantee that the elements of the block are stored in contiguous memory. This allows us to treat a pointer into a `Block` as if it were a pointer into an array, making it easier to use `Blocks` with functions that accept pointers to regular C++ arrays:

```
int sum_of_ints(int*, int count);
// ...
int sum = sum_of_ints(&fib[0], 40);
```

The result of any call to `operator[]` is guaranteed to be valid until the next call to `size(int)`. Calling `operator[]` with an index greater than or equal to the `size()` will have undefined behavior; since run time performance is our primary goal, we do not want to pay the run time cost of checking each access.

8.2.1   Implementing `Block`

The implementation of `Block` is straightforward: we maintain a pointer to a contiguous array of Ts and a count. For performance reasons, we make everything except the resize operation inline:

```
template <class T>
class Block {
private:
    T*  elements;
    int n_elements;
public:
    Block(int n_elem = 0)
        : elements(new T[n_elem]), n_elements(n_elem) {}
    ~Block() { delete [] elements; }
    void size(int);
    int size() { return n_elements; }
    T& operator[](int indx) { return elements[indx]; }
};
```

The constructor **news** an array of Ts, and initializes the count of the number of elements. The destructor **deletes** the array of elements. (Note that `n_elem` can be zero, which will cause a **new** of an array of zero elements; this is legal according to the rules of C++.) The [] operator provides element access by calling the built-in C++ [] operator to return a reference to the indexed element.

To set the size, we allocate space for a new array and copy the appropriate objects into it:

```
template <class T>
void
Block<T>::size(int new_sz) {
    if (new_sz != size()) {
        T* new_ele = new T[new_sz];
        if (new_ele == 0)
            fatal_error("Out of memory");
        int n_copy = (new_sz < size())
            ? new_sz : size();

        for (int i = 0; i < n_copy; ++i)
            new_ele[i] = elements[i];

        delete [] elements;
        elements = new_ele;
        n_elements = new_sz;
    }
}
```

If the call to `size(int)` causes the `Block` to grow, we copy all of the elements from the old storage into the new storage. If the `Block` is shrinking, we copy only the elements that will fit (conceptually, the block is truncated, although we do not implement it that way).

Note that we have to copy all of the elements even if the block is shrinking. Shrinking a block must cause the "truncated" objects to be destroyed, but there is no reasonable way to selectively destroy some of the elements of an array.[2] So we have to allocate space for an entire new array, copy the required elements into it, and destroy the entire old array.

8.3   Detailed `Block` design issues

Now that our `Block` template is working, let's look more closely at some details of its design.

---

[2] While we could destroy individual elements by making explicit calls to the destructor, those elements would be destroyed *again* when the array was deleted, with undefined results.

8.3.1 Automatic resize

We start by asking why `operator[]` has undefined behavior when the subscript is too big; why can't it just check the size and grow the `Block` if necessary?

```
// Dangerous enhancement to Block
template <class T>
T&
Block<T>::operator[](int indx) {
    if (indx >= size())
        size(indx+1); // indx is 0 origin
    return elements[indx];
}
```

With this change, the `Block` would grow automatically if an element past the end were referenced; no explicit call to `size` would be needed:

```
Block<int> block;
block[5] = x;
```

There are two reasons why we might not want to do this. With our original implementation, accessing an element of a `Block` is as fast as accessing an element of an array. That would no longer be true with this change, which would violate our primary design goal of maximum run time performance.

The second problem with this change is that any call to `operator[]` could cause a reallocation. This could lead to disaster if `operator[]` was called twice in the same expression:

```
Block<int> ray;
// ...
ray[x] = ray[y]; //unsafe
```

The following sequence of events could happen:

1. `ray[x]` is evaluated, returning a reference (which is really a pointer) to the location of the xth element of `ray`.

2. Then `ray[y]` is evaluated, which causes a reallocation. All of the elements of `ray` are copied into the new area, and the old elements are deleted.

3. The assignment is done, copying `ray[y]` into the memory that `ray[x]` used to occupy (instead of the new location of `ray[x]`). Chaos results.

Here is another example:

```
void walk_sequence(int* start, int* end);
walk_sequence(&ray[0], &ray[10]);
```

If `ray[0]` is evaluated first, and the subsequent evaluation of `ray[10]` real-locates the array, the first argument to `walk_sequence` will point at deleted memory. This is especially nasty since the evaluation order of function arguments in C++ is undefined; a change in compiler implementation strategy (or a port to a new compiler) could cause this bug to surface in previously working code.

Things are easier for the container implementor if there is no way to get a pointer or reference into a container; but such pointers or references are often necessary in practice. This may be to avoid the cost of copying the elements of the container, or the logic of the program may not allow the object to be copied. If a container does provide operations that return pointers or references into itself, the interface of the container should specify how long those values are guaranteed to remain valid. Operations like the automatically resizing version of `operator[]` whose returned values are valid "until the next time this operation is called" should be avoided. Even if we carefully document this behavior, there are too many chances for mysterious bugs that appear only when expressions are evaluated in a certain order.

With our original `Block` class, we do not have this problem, since the result of `operator[]` is valid until the next call to `size(int)` on that `Block`. Of course, the tradeoff is that user code must worry about when to grow the `Block`.

8.3.2   Performance in common situations

Whenever you build a container, consider the performance characteristics of its use in common situations. The two most common situations are the initial population of the container and iteration through the container.

Let's consider how someone might populate a `Block`. Suppose that we are using a `Block` to store a stream of input, and we do not know in advance how long that stream would be. The obvious way to do this is to grow the `Block` as necessary:

```
extern int gets(String&); // Read a line into a String
main() {
    Block<String> input;
    String line;
    int line_no = 0;

    while(gets(line)) {
        input.size(line_no+1);
        input[line_no++] = line;
    }
```

This code works, but it is very slow. The problem is that resizing a `Block` involves copying all the elements, so that the cost of a call to `size(int)` is $O(size())$. Since this loop does a resize at every iteration, the run time of the loop is quadratic on the size of the input.

One solution is to add a `reserve` function that puts a lower bound, but no upper bound, on the size of the `Block`:

```
while(gets(line)) {
    input.reserve(line_no+1);
    input[line_no++] = line;
}
```

If `input` has at least `line_no+1` elements, this call has no effect. Otherwise, `input` will be grown to *at least* `line_no+1` elements; but it can be more. The actual amount the `Block` grows is an implementation detail.

By allowing the `Block` to grow by more than one element, we can arrange for loops that populate a `Block` to have linear time. Here is one possible implementation of `reserve`:

```
template <class T>
void
Block<T>::reserve(int sz) {
    int new_sz = (size() == 0) ? 1 : size();
    while(new_sz < sz)
        new_sz *= 2;
    size(new_sz);
}
```

If the `Block` has to grow, it will grow by *doubling* its size (or by increasing it to one if the `Block` has a zero size). This way, most calls to `reserve` will not cause a reallocation. We adjust our guarantee on pointers or references into the block to say that such pointers or references are valid until the next call to `size(int)` or `reserve(int)`.

If we use `reserve` to fill the `Block`, the total number of reallocations is $O(\log_2 \texttt{size}())$, and the total number of copies of `T` is bounded by

$$n + \frac{n}{2} + \frac{n}{4} + \frac{n}{8} + \ldots + 0$$

where n is the maximum size of the `Block`; we can rewrite this expression as

$$n(1 + \frac{1}{2} + \frac{1}{4} + \frac{1}{8} + \ldots + 0)$$

which must be less than $2n$; this means that the time to fill a `Block` is linear on the size of the block.

We should also consider the performance of iteration through a `Block`. Since a call to `operator[]` expands inline to a simple array reference, iteration through a `Block` should be as fast as iteration through an array.

8.3.3   Common coding idioms

We would like the code for the most common uses of our container to be as terse as possible. If you look back through the code to populate a loop using `reserve`, you will see that every call to `reserve(int)` includes a `+1` to convert a zero-origin value to a one-origin value. How can we avoid this extra addition?

One approach is to change the definition of `reserve` so that a call to `reserve(n)` ensures that there are at least `n+1` elements in the `Block`. The code to fill a block now reads like this:

```
while(gets(line)) {
    input.reserve(line_no);
    input[line_no++] = line;
}
```

We are willing to introduce this wrinkle only because the consequences of a user forgetting about it are small. If a user passes the `+1` anyway, the program will still get the right answer: the `Block` may just be a little larger than it had to be.

8.3.4   Collision with built-in types

When designing templates with overloaded functions, be alert for the possibility of certain template arguments causing duplicate function declarations. For instance, we might try to add some extra `Block` constructors to allow users to create small `Blocks` with some of their elements already initialized:

```
template <class T>
// Dangerous enhancement for Block
class Block {
public:
    Block(int n); // "n" elements with default value

    Block(T); // Block containing one element
    Block(T, T); // Block containing two elements
    Block(T, T, T); // Block containing three elements
// other details omitted
};
```

This would allow code like

```
Block<String> names("Jane", "Doe");
```

which creates a two-element `Block`.

This seems to work until someone tries to instantiate a `Block<int>`; that user gets an instantiation error, because there are two declarations of `Block<int>::Block(int)`!

You can get around this by providing a specialization for `Block<int>` (see Section 8.8), but the result is still confusing; is

```
Block<int> b(4);
```

a one element block containing a 4, or an uninitialized four element block? It is better to avoid the confusion by not supplying the extra constructors.

8.4   Containers with iterators: a List class

Our `Block` class uses integers to support iteration through the container. That works fine for `Blocks`, which can grow or shrink only at one end, since the same integer is guaranteed to refer to the same element as long as it is in the container.

Integers do not work as well for containers that can add or remove elements somewhere other than at the end, since adding or removing an element changes the indices of the subsequent elements. Integers also do not work if the container does not model a one-dimensional sequence of elements; for instance, it would be awkward to use integers to iterate over a tree. It is better to provide a separate *iterator* object for such containers. In this section, we will design a `List` class template, and an accompanying `Listiter` iterator. A `List` will be homogeneous, have value semantics, and contain objects of any copyable type. For simplicity, we only allow movement forward through the `List`, not backward.

The List interface

The `List`[3] class has almost no interface:

```
template <class T>
class List {
// details omitted
public:
        List();
    int length() const;
};
```

To provide access to individual list elements, we need an *iterator* class. We will define a `Listiter` as an object that (conceptually) points *between* two elements of a `List`—or it can point before the first element or after the last element (see Fig. 8.1).

List elements

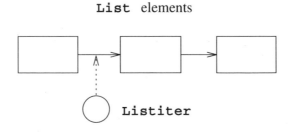

Figure 8.1: List iterators

---

[3]This class is modeled after the `List` class from the USL Standard Components; the original version was designed by Jonathan Shopiro.

`Listiter` provides all of the operations that depend on the position in a list:

```
template <class T>
class Listiter {
// details omitted
public:
    Listiter(List<T>&);
    ~Listiter();

    void insert_after(const T&);
    void remove_after();

    int next(T&);
    int peek_next(T&);
};
```

A `Listiter` must always be initialized with a reference to the `List` it iterates over:

```
List<Thing> list;
// populate the list...
Listiter<Thing> iter(list);
```

Once created, a `Listiter` cannot be changed to point at any other List.

We put this functionality in a separate class (as opposed to putting it in `List`), because we would like it to be possible for two or more iterations to be pending on the same `List`. Operations that change the position of one iterator should not affect the other. (An insertion or removal, however, should be immediately visible to all iterators on a `List`.)

Iterators: between or at elements?

Having the iterators conceptually point between elements has an important benefit: when an element is inserted or removed, the behavior of iterators in the immediate vicinity becomes obvious. If an iterator conceptually pointed directly at an object and that object was removed from the list, what would happen to the iterator—would it point at the previous object or the next? If the iterator points between two objects, we avoid this problem.

On the other hand, with this model, any iterator operation that affects an existing object must specify whether the operation affects the object before the iterator or after it. Iterators that point directly at an object avoid this problem, although their "insert" operations must still specify whether the object is to be inserted before or after the current object.

When designing a family of containers, consistency is more important than the merits of one model over the other; whichever model you choose, you should stick with it over the entire family.

Other iterator functions

The `next` function is used to step through the `List`. If the iterator is not at the end of the list, a call to `next` will copy the element after the iterator into the location referenced by the argument to `next`, step the iterator so that it points after that argument, and return 1. Otherwise `next` will return 0, ignoring its argument. This supports the idiom

```
Listiter<Thing> iter(/* ... */);
Thing t;
while(iter.next(t)) {
    // use t
}
```

The `peek_next` function will have the same semantics as `next`, except that it will not step the iterator. The `insert_after` function will insert its argument into the list, leaving the iterator pointing before the new element. The `remove_after` function will remove the argument after the iterator; it will raise an error if the iterator is at the end of the `List`.

This is a minimal interface; a production `List` class should contain more functionality (see question 9).

Implementing `List`

The `List` object will contain a pointer to the head of a chain of `List_links`, each of which will contain a pointer to the next element in the list, and the actual contained object (see Fig. 8.2).

Let's design our `List_link` class; since it is an implementation class, all of its members will be private, and `List` will be a friend. A `List_link<T>` has two data members: a pointer to the next link in the list, and the `T` list element.

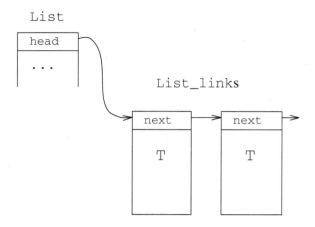

Figure 8.2: List implementation

```
template <class T> class List;
template <class T> class Listiter;
template <class T>
class List_link {
    friend class List<T>;
    friend class Listiter<T>;
private:
    List_link<T>*      next;
    T                  data;
    List_link(const T&, List_link<T>*);
};
```

The `List_link` constructor just initializes the data members:

```
template <class T>
List_link<T>::List_link(const T& val, List_link<T>* nxt)
: data(val),  next(nxt) {
}
```

Next, we write the `List` class; each `List` will contain a pointer to the first `List_link` and a count of the number of elements on the `List`. (We discuss the function of the `iters` member when we get to the `Listiter` class):

```
template <class T>
class List {
friend class List_link<T>;
friend class Listiter<T>;
private:
    List_link<T>*      head;
    Set<Listiter<T>*>  iters;
    int                n_elem;
public:
                       List();
    int                length() const { return n_elem; }
};
```

The `List` constructor creates an empty `List`.

```
template <class T>
List<T>::List()
: head(0),
  n_elem(0) {
}
```

Next, we implement the iterators. Although our abstract model states that `Listiter`s point between two objects, we implement them as pointers that point *at* an object, since C++ does not support pointers "between" things. We assume that the pointer points at the previous object; if the iterator is at the head of the list, the pointer will be zero.

If a `Listiter` really points at an object, what happens if that object is removed from the `List`? The pointer must be updated to point at the *previous* object (or zeroed if the removed object was at the head of the List). Since two or more iterators may be pointing at the removed object, `remove_after` must check *every* `Listiter` on the `List` to see if it needs to be adjusted. To support this, each `List` maintains a `Set` of pointers to all of the `Listiter`s currently iterating on it.

Each `Listiter` contains a pointer to the `List` it iterates on and a pointer to the "previous" object (the object conceptually "before" the iterator):

```
template <class T>
class Listiter {
private:
    List_link<T>*    prev;
    List<T>*         the_list;
    List_link<T>**   next_link();
public:
    Listiter(List<T>&);
    Listiter(const Listiter<T>&);
    ~Listiter();

    void insert_after(const T&);
    void remove_after();

    int next(T&);
    int peek_next(T&);
};
```

The `Listiter` constructors and destructor must update the `Set` of current iterators:

```
template <class T>
Listiter<T>::Listiter(List<T>& list)
: prev(0),
  the_list(&list) {
    the_list->iters.insert(this);
}

template <class T>
Listiter<T>::Listiter(const Listiter<T>& iter)
: prev(iter.prev),
  the_list(iter.the_list) {
    the_list->iters.insert(this);
}

template <class T>
Listiter<T>::~Listiter() {
    the_list->iters.remove(this);
}
```

This next (private) function will come in handy when implementing the other `Listiter` functions; it returns the *address* of the pointer that points at the

List_link after the iterator:

```
template <class T>
List_link<T>**
Listiter<T>::next_link() {
    if (prev)
        return &(prev->next);
    else
        return &(the_list->head);
}
```

Here, insert_after creates a new List_link, inserts it into the chain, and updates the count of list elements:

```
template <class T>
void
Listiter<T>::insert_after(const T& ele) {
    // Insert the new link

    List_link<T>** nextlink = next_link();
    *nextlink = new List_link<T>(ele, *nextlink);

    // Update the count of list elements

    the_list->n_elem++;
}
```

remove_after removes the List_link from the chain and updates the count of list elements; but it must also notify all of the existing iterators on the List being changed:

```
template <class T>
void
Listiter<T>::remove_after() {

    // Find the link to be removed
    List_link<T>* removed;
    List_link<T>** nextlink = next_link();
    removed = *nextlink;
    if (!removed)
        internal_error("Remove from end of list");

    // Remove the link
    *nextlink = removed->next;
```

```
    /* Find all iterators that point after "removed" and
       fix them to point after "prev";
       See footnote* if using Set
       from USL Standard Components library */

    Setiter<Listiter<T>*> listiters(the_list->iters);
    Listiter<T>* iter;
    while(listiters.next(iter)) {
        if (iter->prev == removed)
            iter->prev = prev;
    }

    // delete the removed link
    delete removed;

    // Update the count of list elements
    the_list->n_elem--;
}
```

The `peek_next` function examines the next element without changing the state of the iterator:

```
template <class T>
int
Listiter<T>::peek_next(T& ele) {
    List_link<T>** nextlink = next_link();
    if (*nextlink == 0)
        return 0;
    ele = (*nextlink)->data;
    return 1;
}
```

---

* If you are using the Set class from the USL Standard Components, a Setiter returns a *pointer* into the Set, so the last loop of **remove_after** should be

```
Listiter<T>** piter;
while(listiters.next(piter))
{
    if ((*piter)->prev == removed)
        (*piter)->prev = prev;
}
```

`next` calls `peek_next` to get the next value and steps the iterator before returning:

```
template <class T>
int
Listiter<T>::next(T& ele) {
    if (peek_next(ele)) {
        prev = *(next_link());
        return 1;
    }
    return 0;
}
```

Getting these functions right takes some care on the part of the `List` implementor; but once they are right, the user does not have to worry about them.

8.5   Iterator design issues

Let's look at some of the interactions between iterators and their containers.

8.5.1   Updating iterators when the container changes or is destroyed

When a container is changed (i.e., an element is added or removed), all of the iterators active on that container must be notified. Our `List` class remembers all of the active iterators in its `iters` member. When an iterator changes the `List`, it checks every other iterator on that `List` to see if it is affected by the change. There may also be iterators pointing into a container when it is destroyed. Further references through those iterators should do something sensible, such as throw an exception or act as if they were pointing into an empty container.

Here is an alternative for containers whose iterators conceptually point at, rather than between, elements: if an element that is removed from a container has one or more iterators pointing at it, the element is not destroyed until all of the iterators pointing at it are destroyed. The iterators maintain use counts in the elements. The disadvantage to this strategy is that every time an iterator is stepped, it must adjust the use counts in the objects.

8.5.2   next() design

Iteration through a container is a common operation, so the **next** function should be as terse (to minimize typing) and as fast as possible. This is complicated by the fact that **next** conceptually returns two values: a flag indicating whether the operation succeeded and, if it did, the value of the next object. One choice might be to return a **Pair<int,T>**; but an iteration using that design would look like this:

```
Listiter<Thing> iter;
Pair<int,Thing> rc;
while(rc = iter.next(), rc.left()) {
  // ...
```

which in this case is not nearly as terse as returning the T object by storing through a reference:

```
Listiter<Thing> iter;
Thing val;
while(iter.next(val)) {
    // ...
```

For most types this second alternative works well. However, for each iteration, the user must first create an empty T that is then assigned to by next. This can be a problem if there is no default constructor for T.

We would like our template to work with as many classes as possible. So, in anticipation of users who want to use our template with classes that have no default constructor, we can supply an alternative form of **next**. If pointers into the container are supported, the alternative **next** can "return" a pointer to the next item:

```
template <class T>
class Listiter {
public:
// ...
    int next(T&);
    int next(T*&);
};
```

Of course, the valid lifetime of the pointer "returned" by **next(T*&)** must be specified. Since we do not move objects around once they have been put

into a `List_link`, we can guarantee that the pointer will be valid as long as
the element is in the `List`.

If pointers into containers are not supported, it may be best to split the
test and next functions:

```
template <class T>
class Listiter {
public:
// ...
    int next(T&);
    T   next();
    int at_end();
};
```

The `next()` function will return a `T`, but this allows us no way to signal the
end of the `List`. For this, we add the `at_end` function, which will return
1 if and only if the iterator is pointing after the last element of the list.
The `next()` function (but not the `next(T&)` function) will raise an error (by
throwing an exception, if using a version of C++ that supports them) if it is
called when `at_end()` is true.

Code that uses these two functions would look like this:

```
Listiter<Thing> iter(/* ... */);
while(!iter.at_end()) {
    Thing t(iter.next());
    // ...
}
```

This is not as terse as the original iteration, but it does not involve the
creation of an empty `Thing` or a function returning a pointer into the `List`.

8.5.3   Const iterators

The `Listiter` constructor takes a `List<T>&`, not a `const List<T>&`. This
is because the iterator can change the `List` by calling `insert_after` or
`remove_after`.

We might want to also provide a `Const_listiter` that can iterate over
a const `List`. The constructor for a `Const_listiter` would take a `const`
`List<T>&`—but there would be no `insert_after` or `replace_after` members, since these would change the `List`. Once we have const `Lists`, we can

declare functions that take `const List&` arguments; these functions can use `Const_listiter`s to examine, but not change, those arguments:

```
void
examine(const List<int>& list) {
    Const_listiter<int> iter(list);
    int i;
    while (iter.next(i))
        // etc...
```

The caller of `examine` knows that the `List` argument will not be modified in that function.

A `Listiter` can do anything a `Const_listiter` can do, and then some; so `Listiter` should be derived from `Const_listiter`. (A `Listiter` is-a `Const_listiter` that can also change the `List`.) We put the inquiry functions in `Const_listiter`, and the insertion and removal functions in `Listiter`:

```
template <class T>
class Const_listiter {
private:
    List_link<T>*    prev;
    List<T>*         the_list;
public:
    Const_listiter(const List<T>&);
    virtual ~Const_listiter();

    int next(T&);
    int peek_next(T&);
};

template <class T>
class Listiter : public Const_listiter<T> {
public:
    Listiter(List<T>&);
    ~Listiter();

    void insert_after(const T&);
    void remove_after();
};
```

The inheritance is public (it is part of the interface); this allows us to pass a `Listiter&` to a function that takes a `Const_listiter&` argument.

An attempt to attach a `Listiter` to a `const List&` will fail (because the `Listiter` constructor takes a nonconst reference). An attempt to change a list through a `Const_listiter` will also fail, because those functions are not declared in that class. Of course, you can defeat this scheme by casting a const reference to a nonconst reference; but that is true with const in general.

Every feature has costs: in development time, in code size and performance, and in ease of understanding. Are const iterators worth it? For a small template with local use, it may not be worth the bother. For a template that will be widely used (like `List`) it is probably worthwhile. Like most of the interesting questions in C++, it is a judgment call.

8.6   Performance issues

Templates make it easier for programmers to use lots of new classes without writing them, but they do not make the compiler's job any easier. The compile time overhead of template instantiation can be significant for a large program. This section contains a couple of techniques that can lower the burden on the compiler.

8.6.1   Coalescing common logic

Some general purpose containers such as `List` can be expected to be instantiated multiple times in a single program. When designing such a template, look for opportunities to coalesce code that is independent of the type arguments into a single place, so that all instantiations of the template can share a single copy of that code. This avoids the compile time cost of compiling the code for every instantiation, and the program space cost of having multiple copies of the code in a running program.

The most common opportunities for coalescing involve operations that manipulate pointers without knowing anything about the pointed-to object. Such operations can often be implemented using `void*`s. The code that manipulates the `void*`s is shared, with the results of those operations cast back to their actual types by (unshared) logic in the class template.

For example, every `List<T>` contains a `Set<Listiter<T>*>`, so the compiler will have to instantiate a different `Set` class for every `List` instantiation. To avoid this, we change `List` to maintain a `Set<void*>` instead of a `Set<Listiter<T>*>`:

```
template <class T>
class List {
friend class List_link<T>;
friend class Listiter<T>;
private:
    List_link<T>*      head;
    Set<void*>         iters;
public:
                       List();
    int                length() const;
};
```

Operations that retrieve pointers from the Set must now cast them back to
Listiter<T>*:[4]

```
template <class T>
void
Listiter<T>::remove_after() {
// ...
    Setiter<void*> listiters(the_list->iters);
    void* iter;
    while(listiters.next(iter)) {
        if (((Listiter<T>*)iter)->prev == removed)
            ((Listiter<T>*)iter)->prev = prev;
// ...
}
```

We have muddied our code a bit, but the benefit is that all of the Lists in
a program now share the instantiation of Set<void*>.

We should not do this for every container, of course. By using void*, the
implementation loses the benefit of some static type checking and becomes
harder to understand. We have to balance this against the anticipated gain,
which depends on how many times List will be instantiated in a typical
program, and the cost of each extra Set instantiation. If either of these
values is small, it may not be worth it to coalesce the common logic.

If we wanted to coalesce even more, we could have every template class
derive from a common (nontemplate) base class that contains the logic that

---

[4]Unlike ANSI C, there is no implicit conversion from void* to any other pointer in
C++. To convert a void* to another pointer you must supply an explicit cast.

is independent of T:

```
/* Common logic for list links: */
class List_link_base {
private:
    List_link_base* next;
// ...
};

/* T-specific logic: */
template <class T>
class List_link : public List_link_base {
private:
    T data;
// ...
};
```

The code to maintain the **next** pointer is in class **List_link_base**; only the T-specific code would be in the **List_link** template. **List** and **Listiter** would also have to be split in this fashion.

You should do this only if space expansion becomes a serious problem; splitting a container into type-independent and type-specific parts makes things a lot more complicated.

8.6.2   All-inline templates

Instantiation time is one of the major costs of using a template; if all of the member functions of a template are inline, instantiation times are no longer an issue. You should still avoid making large functions inline—the extra space and compile time is likely to outweigh any savings in templates instantiation. However, when designing a template, you should try a little harder to make all of the member functions inline.

8.7   Constraints on template arguments

Templates are most powerful when the logic for the template is largely independent of the template argument. For instance, the logic to manage a stack of **ints** and a stack of **char*s** is the same; a template lets us write only one implementation of that logic. However, many templates place *some* requirements on their type arguments.

For example, assume that there is a `List::max()` function that finds the largest element of a list, using the < operator for comparison:

```
template <class T>
T
List<T>::max() {
    Listiter<T> iter(*this);

    T biggest;

    /* initialize "biggest" with the value of the
       first element. */

    if (iter.next(biggest) == 0)
        internal_error("max of empty list");

    /* Iterate through remaining elements, if any, and
       remember the largest element. */

    T ele;
    while(iter.next(ele))
        if (biggest < ele)
            biggest = ele;

    return biggest;
};
```

This function will compile only if there is a default constructor for T, two Ts can be compared using <, and two Ts can be assigned. An attempt to find the `max` of a `List` of T's for which any of these operations does not compile will cause an instantiation error.

We should be precise about what is required of type T. There need not be an **operator<** that takes two T arguments; it is necessary only that the code fragment

```
if (biggest < ele)
```

compiles cleanly. For instance:

```
class Number_string {
// details omitted
public:
    Number_string(const char*);
    operator int();
};
```

Even if there is no `operator<(Number_string,Number_string)`, we can still call `List<Number_string>::max`. This is because applying the `<` operator to a pair of `Number_strings` will cause each `Number_string` to be implicitly converted to `int`, and the resulting `ints` compared.

Templates are like macros in that the real meaning of a template is unknown until it is instantiated. In particular, you do not know until instantiation time whether a given instantiation will even compile and, if it does, what other templates it needs. The provider of the `List` class should document the requirements of the `max` function.

8.7.1   Different member functions may have different constraints

According to the rules of C++, it is OK to use a template even if one or more of its member functions will not instantiate—*as long as those member functions are not used.* This means that it is not right to say `List<T>` requires comparison using `<`; rather, `List<T>::max` requires comparison using `<`. You can use a `List` with objects that cannot be compared with `<` as long as you never call `max` on the `List`.

There are two caveats to this rule. First, all virtual functions in a class template are treated as "called"; if a class template is used, all of its virtual functions must instantiate successfully. Second, some compiler implementations always instantiate all the members of the template, rather than just the members that are used. If you are using one of these compilers, you will get an instantiation error if any members do not compile, whether or not you use them.

More constraint examples

Certain templates impose the constraint that a type argument must be a class:

```
template <class T>
class Persistent : public T {
// details omitted
};
```

Unless there is a specialization (see Section 8.8), there can be no `Persistent <int>`, since `int` cannot be a base class. Here is another example:

```
template <class T>
class Smart_pointer {
public:
    T operator->();
};
```

Here, T must either be a pointer to a class, or a class object for which operator-> is declared.

As we have seen, the interface to a class template is more complex than the interface to a regular class. In addition to an abstract model and a list of the available member functions, the interface should also specify any other constraints on the type arguments.

8.8   Template specializations

A template tells the compiler how to build an infinite set of classes (or functions); but this can be overridden for any individual instantiation by defining a *specialization*.

8.8.1   Specializing for performance

Template specializations are often used to provide an alternative implementation for a particular set of type arguments. In the case of our List class, the default List<char> will work correctly, but a faster version might be implemented by storing lists of chars in contiguous memory. Insertions and deletions would involve copying some or all of the list elements, but that is relatively cheap for chars:

```
template <class T>
class List { /* as before */ };

class List<char> {
friend class Listiter<char>;
private:
    char* data;
    int len;
public:
    List();
    int length() const { return len; }
};
```

Noninline member functions (and static data members) of specializations must be defined once in every program, just like any other class:

```
// File List_special.c
#include <List.h>

List<char>::List()
: data(0), len(0)
{}
```

`Listiter<char>` will also have to be specialized to work with the specialized `List<char>`.

There is no requirement that a specialized class must look anything like the general class template with the same name. Nonetheless, a specialization should have the same public interface as the general class template. If the interface is different, why do you want the class to be called a `List`?

8.8.2   Specializing to get around a template constraint

Specializations can also be used when a particular argument type violates a constraint of the general class template. For instance,

```
template <class T>
class Persistent : public T {
// ...
};

class Persistent<int> {
// ...
};

class Persistent<char> {
// ...
};
// And so on ....
```

Here, the default `Persistent` template has the constraint that the type argument must be a class. We get around this for the built-in types by providing specializations. (This does not completely solve the problem, of course, since there are an infinite number of built-in types; the interface to `Persistent` should allow users to write their own specializations when necessary.)

Sometimes you may need to supply specializations only for member functions that would otherwise not compile. The compiler should discover the specialized member functions at link time and refrain from building instantiations for them.

8.8.3   Specializing template functions

Unlike class templates, the template arguments to a template function are not explicitly specified when the template function is called; instead, they are inferred from the types of the actual arguments:

```
template <class T>
void swap(T& left, T& right) {
// details omitted
};


String s,t;
swap(s,t); // Call swap(String&, String&) template
```

You specialize a template function simply by defining a function that matches the template. In this case, any function named **swap** that takes two arguments that are both references to the same type is a specialization of our **swap** template:

```
void swap(String& l, String& r) {
// Specialization code to swap Strings
}
```

Now for the catch: our **swap(String&,String&)** function is treated as a specialization of our **swap** template, even if the **swap** template declaration is not in scope where that function is defined! According to the current language rules, the compiler is obliged to treat *any* function definition in a program that matches a template function specification as a specialization of that function template. This means that a call to a template function that happens to match a function definition in a library will not result in a loader error; the function in the library will be treated as a specialization instead.

Consider an operating system application:

```
/* Set up two file systems for swapping:
   primary and backup */
void
swap(String& primary, String& backup) {
    // Complicated logic to manipulate file systems
}
```

If we link an object file that (apparently) calls the `swap` template on `Strings` with a library containing the definition of this function, we will call this function instead, with mysterious results.

It is best to avoid situations like this by not using function templates heavily, and by avoiding common names like `read` or `write`.

8.8.4   Specializations and inline functions

The C++ language rules require that a specialization be used if it is defined anywhere in the program; this means that the compiler cannot perform any template instantiations until link time, since a specialization can be discovered in a library. There is one exception to this: an inline function may be expanded at compile time, even if a specialization of that function is discovered later (at link time). The safest way to suppress this is to declare the specialization class before any calls to member functions of that class:

```
template <class T>
class List {
public:
    int length() const { return len; }
// details omitted ...
};

class List<char>{
public:
    int length() const; // not inline for some reason
// ... details omitted
};

void walk(List<char>& list) {
    int i = list.length(); // Calls the (noninline)
                           // List<char>::length()
```

8.8.5   User-supplied specializations

The template designer may require each template user to write a specialization that provides some type-specific functionality in the template argument. For example, a Set<T> template might require a hash function on Ts. The performance of the Set depends to a great extent on the performance and quality of the hash function; but there is no way to write a good hash function that works for all types. An algorithm that works well for void*'s might not work so well for Strings. Each user of this class will therefore have to write a hash function for each T.

One approach is to declare the hash function in the template as a static member function, but never provide a definition of it:

```
template <class T> class Set {
public:
  // details omitted
  static unsigned hash(const T&);
};
```

Users of Sets will get loader errors:

```
Undefined Set<String>::hash(const String&)
```

unless one of the object files provides a specialization of the hash function:

```
#include <String.h>

unsigned
Set<String>::hash(const String& f) {
  // ....
}
```

The provider of Set might provide a default hash function; but since we know nothing about T, about the only thing this hash function can use is the address of its operand:

```
template <class T>
unsigned
Set<T>::hash(const T& t) {
    return (unsigned)(&t);
}
```

This allows a Set to be used even if the hash function is not defined; but the performance may suffer, since taking the address may not be a good hash function for a particular T. It is a judgment call: the convenience of being able to use Sets right away (delaying the design of the hash function until later) must be weighed against the possibility that users will forget to go back and write the hash functions.

The user of a class that requires a user-supplied specialization must understand how to write a specialization and must remember to do so for every use of the template. There are alternatives that do not impose this burden.

Constructor arguments

You might arrange for the user of a template to supply the hash function as an argument to the constructor:

```
template <class T>
class Set {
public:
    Set(unsigned (*HASH)(const T&));
// ...
};

// ...

extern unsigned hash(const Thing&);

Set<Thing> tset(hash);
```

There are some drawbacks. The user must specify the hash function whenever a Set is created; and every call of hash is done through a pointer, which means that hash cannot be expanded inline.

Expression arguments

We might decide that the hash function could be an expression argument to the template:

```
template <class T, unsigned (*HASH)(const T&)>
class Set {
public:
    Set();
// ...
};
```

```
extern unsigned hash(const Thing&);
Set<Thing,hash> tset;
```

This preserves the ability to call the hash function inline, but now we have to specify the hash function every time the Set class is even mentioned! In practice, the user would be forced to invent a new name and use a typedef:

```
typedef Set<Thing,hash> Thing_set;
```

Not only is it a bother to force users to invent new names, it makes the code less clear, especially if the users do not use a consistent naming convention. It is obvious that a Set<Foo> and Set<Bar> are closely related; but what about Thing_set and Set_of_Things? Is this a duplication or are these two classes different in some subtle way?

Pure virtual function

There is one more choice: the template could declare (but not define) a pure virtual function that provides the functionality.

```
template <class T>
class Set {
public:
    Set();
    virtual unsigned hash(const T&) = 0;
// ...
};
```

The user must then derive from Set<T> and provide a definition of the hash function:

```
class Thing_set : public Set<Thing> {
public:
    unsigned hash(const Thing&);
};

unsigned
Thing_set::hash(const Thing& t) {
// ...
}
```

This allows the user to have two or more sets of Things that use different hash functions in the same program. On the other hand, more baggage must be supplied by the user, including the invention of a new name for every new version of `Set`; and every call to `hash` will be a virtual function call.

8.8.6   Which alternative is best?

The main advantage of these alternatives to specialization is that they allow a program to contain two or more sets of `Things` that use different hash functions. In the case of our `Set` class, we reject these solutions because we anticipate that all `Set<T>`s in a program will use the same hash function for a given type `T`. (If this were not the case, we could not use user-supplied specializations.) The user-supplied specialization lets the user specify the hash function once in the program and then forget about it.

Suppose a particular template needs user-supplied functionality, but that functionality is expected to vary from object to object? If we anticipate that each object will have its own unique functionality, then passing a function pointer to the constructor seems the best choice, since the other schemes all involve making a new class for each user-supplied function. If the functionality is provided as a small, performance critical function that we would like to have called inline, then we can supply that function as a template expression argument. Otherwise, the derivation from a common base class is simpler and easier to understand (more C++ programmers will understand virtual functions than expression arguments to templates).

8.9   In short

- A container implemented with templates should be homogeneous. The effect of a heterogeneous container can be attained by using a container of pointers (possibly "smart pointers") to a common base class.

- The valid lifetime of a pointer or reference into a container should be specified by the provider of the container. The ideal lifetime is "until the container is destroyed"; a lifetime of "until the next call to this operation" should be avoided.

- Iterators should either point between elements or at elements. A collection of containers should be consistent in this regard.

- All iterators into a container should be updated when the container is changed or destroyed.

- Each member of a template may impose constraints on the template arguments.

- Commonly used templates may benefit from having common logic coalesced and shared by all instantiations.

- Templates may be specialized. A specialization may be discovered at link time.

8.10   Questions

1. C++ has **new** to replace **malloc** and **delete** to replace **free**.   What about **realloc**? Is it safe to use the C function? If not, how can you use a class to get the same functionality?

2. Our **Block** class allows expressions of the form

   ```
   &blk[x]
   ```

   but not

   ```
   blk+x
   ```

   How would you enhance it to allow users to write the second expression as a synonym for the first? (Hint: the expression

   ```
   blk
   ```

   ought to be legal also.)

3. Design an alternative to **Block** that has safety, not run time performance, as its primary design goal. How did you change the design? What impact did this have on performance?

4. Design an alternative to **Block** that supports automatic resizing in a safe manner, so that

   ```
   blk[x] = blk[y];
   ```

   will be safe even if one of the references causes the container to be reallocated. What characteristics of the original **Block** class did you have to sacrifice to make this possible?

5. What is wrong with this `Pair` template?

```
template <class Left, class Right>
class Pair {
// details omitted
public:
    Pair(const Left& l, const Right& r);
    Left left();
    void set(const Left&);
    Right right();
    void set(const Right&);
};
```

6. Under what circumstances might a loop that populates a `Block` actually become slower by doing a `reserve` instead of a `size` for every element?

7. If `Block::reserve` decides to grow the `Block`, it grows it by a factor of two. What other strategies might you use for `reserve`? (Hint: consider the performance when filling a small block. Another hint: consider the implications on `malloc` when filling a large block.)

8. Enhance the `Block` class so that it is usable with objects that have a constructor but no default constructor.

9. What functions would you add to the `List` template to make it a production class that you would use for your projects? Defend your choices (and your omissions). What impact will the new functions have on performance? On understandability?

10. Our `List` class does not update the iterators when the `List` is destroyed. For each `Listiter` member function, decide on the semantics if that function is called after the `List` is destroyed, and implement your suggestion.

11. Instead of introducing the `Listiter::at_end` function (see page 186), we might try returning an integer through a reference argument that will be zero when we reach the end of the list:

```
template <class T>
class Listiter {
public:
// ...
    int next(T&); // Normal form
    T   next(int&); /* Form when there is no
                       default constructor for T */
};
```

What is wrong with this design?

12. The USL Standard Components library includes a Set_of_p template; a Set_of_p<T> is essentially the same as a Set<T*>. Suggest one reason why this might be a good idea.

13. Our specialization of List<char> will have the property that an insertion into the list, or deletion from the list, may rearrange the list. What potential incompatibility does this introduce with the general List class template?

14. Design and implement a specialized Listiter<char> to work with our specialized List<char> template.

Chapter 9

Reusability

Reuse is one of the best ways to increase programming productivity; not writing new code must always be faster than writing new code, right?

It is not always that easy; reuse involves both costs and benefits. For the reuse of a piece of code (which for convenience we will call a *library*, although it may be a single class or even a single function) to be a win, the benefits must outweigh the costs. Those costs include

- Discovery—the user must select the library from the libraries that are available;

- Acquisition—the user must get a version of the library up and running on his or her system;

- Learning curve—the user must understand the library's abstractions and become familiar with the detailed interface;

- Loss of control—the user no longer has the ability to tinker with the code to make it "just right" for the application.[1] If two libraries interact badly with one another, it may be difficult to resolve the problem;

- Slower turnaround for bug fixes—if a bug is found, the user must coordinate with the provider of the code to get a fix. If there is no workaround, this can be a critical problem;

- Risk—if the library turns out to be a slickly packaged piece of junk, or it is too slow, or the provider does not support it, it may be necessary

---

[1]While this is arguably a benefit, the person who makes the reuse decision may not see it that way.

to tear it out and redo it yourself. This can be disruptive (not to mention frustrating) if it happens late in the development process.

Exacerbating this problem is the fact that developers usually underestimate the cost of building their own version of a library. The *perceived* benefits must be significantly greater than the *perceived* cost of building the code from scratch for the reuse to take place.

Nevertheless, reuse, when it works, is still a good thing. This chapter will discuss some techniques to minimize the costs and raise the benefits, with a focus on these themes:

- **Discovery**—how to make it easier for potential users to discover your library and decide whether it will help them solve their problem;

- **Robustness**—how to make your code "bullet proof," so that it will work even when used in ways you did not anticipate;

- **Name collisions**—how to reduce the chances of collisions between the external names defined by your library and external names defined by other parts of the program;

- **Performance**—how to analyze and tune the space and run time usage of your library.

Memory management is a common source of both bugs and performance problems, so it will be covered in both the Robustness and Performance sections.

9.1   Discovery and acquisition

A programmer ought to be able to quickly decide whether a particular library is useful. If it is, it should be easy to get it up and running.

9.1.1   A simple abstraction

A potential user may read only the first line of your manual page; make it count. You ought to be able to describe your library with a one-line "executive summary" (see page 8). If it takes more than that, your library may be too specialized or may contain too many abstractions bundled into one package. Either way, it is unlikely to be perceived as being easy to pick up and use in an application.

9.1.2   Documentation

Of course there should be a manual page, and it should contain all the information needed to decide whether the library is right for a given task. Someone deciding whether to use the library is unlikely to take the time to read an accompanying tutorial as part of the discovery process. The manual page should be all that is required to use a small library (e.g., a `String` class). For a substantial library (e.g., a complete input-output package), a more extensive tutorial is probably necessary.

9.1.3   Well-chosen class names

Choosing the names of your classes is one of the hardest parts of library design. This is especially true for classes that will be used by someone other than yourself. An apparent disagreement between two developers about the correctness of an abstraction often turns out to be a misunderstanding caused by a confusing or imprecise class name.

The class names are the most important part of your documentation. Be prepared to iterate on them as you would on any other part of the design. One of the benefits of CRC cards (see page 17) is the early socialization of the class names; if a name that seems natural to you does not work for anyone else, you will find that out in the CRC process

9.1.4   Acquisition

Small libraries must be trivial to acquire—a library that is not immediately available is unlikely to be used. This implies that small libraries need to be sold in bunches, so that a purchaser can decide in advance to buy the entire collection in anticipation of some of the libraries being used.

9.2   Robustness

Obviously, a reusable library needs to be as close to bug free as possible, since the cost of dealing with a bug in someone else's code is high. But robustness means more than a lack of bugs. A reusable library should be able to handle demands on it that exceed the expectations of the author, since a successful library will be used in ways the author never dreamed of.

Consider this implementation of a `String` class:

```
class String {
private:
    char* data;
    unsigned char length;
// ...
```

The `length` data member holds the length of the string. While this will work fine in most programs, this class will break if a `String` is ever created whose length will not fit into an `unsigned char`. Claims that it would "never happen" are naïve; some user might decide to read an entire file into a single `String`. This is a perfectly reasonable thing to do, but the implementation is not robust enough for that.

Avoiding size assumptions is one important way to make your code more robust. Here are some others:

9.2.1   Assertions

The `assert` macro is a C tool that is even more important in C++. By default, an `assert` takes one argument and halts the program with a diagnostic if that argument is equal to zero:

```
Node* p = something();
assert(p);
Node* kid = p->child(0);
if (kid)
    assert(kid->parent() == p);
```

All the `assert`s in a compilation unit can be turned off by defining the `NDEBUG` macro:

```
CC -c -DNDEBUG file.c
```

When this is done, all `assert`s become no-ops. This means that an assert is "free," in the sense that it will not affect the performance of the final version of the program if it is built with `NDEBUG` defined.

An object-oriented program tends to have a different structure than a procedural one, and this makes the frequent use of assertions even more important. When a procedural program crashes, it is usually fairly easy to figure out the recent history of the program by walking backward through the current function. That is much harder to do with an object-oriented program, because the functions are usually smaller and the flow of control is more complex (especially in the presence of virtual functions). This makes it important to stop a sick program as soon as possible; if the program staggers on for a while before finally dying, it can be hard to figure out where the damage took place.

Assertions can also be used to enforce preconditions on libraries. If the documentation for a particular function states that its argument must be nonzero, the first thing the function should do is assert that the argument is nonzero. That way, a user who passes a zero gets an immediate assertion failure at the point of call, instead of a crash somewhere in the depths of your library.

Assertions and exceptions

There ought to be a version of **assert** that throws an exception instead of printing a message and dumping core. This is a topic of active study by the ISO/ANSI C++ standards committee; if an assertion that throws exceptions becomes widely available, use it, as it gives the user a chance to catch (and deal with) any errors detected in the library.

Side effects in assert statements

The operand of an **assert** should have no side effects that are required for the correct operation of the program:

```
/* Trip an assertion if this operation fails: */
assert(release_lock() == SUCCEED);
```

When NDEBUG is defined, the test will be suppressed, but so will the call to release_lock()!

Some error checks should not use assert

Assertions can be compiled out using NDEBUG; but there may be some checks that you will always want to perform, regardless of the state of NDEBUG. For instance,

```
char* space = new char[BUFFSIZE];
assert(space);
```

While a thorough testing process might give you the confidence to disable asserts that check for logic errors, there is no way to guarantee that programs will not run out of memory. Unless your memory allocator has been instrumented to throw an exception (or otherwise recover) when it runs out of memory, this is a check you will always want to perform—even in the field. The obvious way to do this is to use a function, not **assert**, when the check is to be done unconditionally:

```
inline void
check(int expr, const String& diag) {
    if (expr == 0) {
        cerr << "Internal error: " << diag << endl;
        abort(); // Or throw exception
    }
}
```

assert and **check** are implemented in different ways. The **assert** macro uses the __FILE__ and __LINE__ preprocessor macros to build a diagnostic message that includes the file and line number where the assertion failed. That approach would not be very useful for **check**; since it is a function, not a macro, the file and line number would always correspond to the definition of **check**, not to the place where **check** was called. Instead, **check** takes a **String** argument that is a diagnostic to be printed when the check fails.

```
void
f() {
    char* space = new char[BUFFSIZE];
    check(space != 0, "Memory allocation");
```

Of course, the caller can still use the __FILE__ and __LINE__ macros to build the diagnostic message if that is desired.

9.2.2   Avoid fixed-sized arrays

Many C programs use fixed-sized arrays, which causes them to break when the input gets too large. C programmers use fixed-sized arrays because it is inconvenient and error prone to use **malloc** and **free**; C++ programmers have no such excuse. Use a container class instead, unless you *know* that the array *must* be big enough.

For instance, this use of an array is reasonable:

```
char* days_of_week[7] = {
    "Sunday",
    "Monday",
    "Tuesday",   // ...
```

since the number of days per week is a known constant that is very unlikely to change. On the other hand, this next program reads employee names from the standard input and uses them to populate an array of MAX_EMPLOYEE Employee objects:

```
const int MAX_EMPLOYEE = 1000;
Employee* employees[MAX_EMPLOYEE];

void
read_employees(istream& in) {
    Employee** next - employees;
    String name;
    while (in >> name) {
        if (next >= &employees[MAX_EMPLOYEE-1])
            internal_error("Too much input");
        *next++ = new Employee(namo);
    }
    *next = 0;
}
```

The value of MAX_EMPLOYEE was probably pulled out of thin air; it is a compromise between making the array large enough to handle all *anticipated* cases, and making it small enough to avoid using too much space. If this library is widely reused, someone else will surely use it in an unanticipated way (such as feeding it the federal payroll), causing it to break.

Another disadvantage is that this program will use MAX_EMPLOYEE * sizeof(Employee*) bytes of memory to hold the pointers to the employees, regardless of how many employees were actually read. It would be better if the program used only the memory required to process its actual input, rather than the memory required to process the maximum allowable input.

Here is the right way to do it. We use our Block class from Chapter 8, but any other container that emulates arrays should work as well:

```
Block<Employee*> employees;
int top_employee = 0;

void
read_employees(istream& in) {
    String name;
    while(in >> name) {
        employees.reserve(top_employee);
        employees[top_employee++] = new Employee(name);
    }
}
```

This version of `read_employees` is simpler and more robust than the version that uses an array, as it will fail only when the program runs out of memory. It is true that the version that uses a `Block` takes more time to read the data, but once the data has been read, the *references* into the `Block` are as fast as references into the array. As it turns out, on my machine the run time cost of the `new` dominates, so the difference in performance between the two versions of `read_employees` was not noticeable.

9.2.3 Debugging versions of programs

Providing debugging versions of the critical functions and classes is another way to help make code robust. The debugging versions attempt to detect insane programs early by performing frequent and extensive sanity checks, regardless of the performance impact. Often these include complete audits of the main data structures. For instance, this routine walks a doubly-linked list and makes sure the pointers between elements are consistent:

```
template <class T>
void
Dllist<T>::audit() {
#ifndef NDEBUG
    Dllist_link_base* ptr = head;
    while (ptr && ptr->next)
        assert(ptr->next->prev == ptr);
#endif
}
```

Any operation that changes the list calls the audit before and after the change:

```
template <class T>
void
Dllistiter<T>::insert_after(const T& t) {
    the_list->audit();
    // Logic to do the insert ...
    the_list->audit();
}
// And so forth ..
```

This ensures that any operation that incorrectly sets the **next** and **prev** pointers will immediately trigger an **assert**. The run time of the audit is proportional to the length of the list, but it should not matter since audits are turned on only during development.

Make sure that the existence of the audit function is clearly documented, so that naïve users do not ship programs with the audits turned on. Also be aware that the audits might change the performance complexity. If an operation that walks a list invokes, at each step, an audit that itself walks the entire list, the operation becomes quadratic. If this gets too expensive, the audits may have to be disabled even during development.

9.2.1 The Linton convention

A function that takes a reference argument can take the address of that argument and store it in some location that persists after the function returns. It is important for the caller to know which functions do this, since the caller must worry about actions that leave the stored pointer dangling. For instance:

```
const Thing* last_accessed_thing;
void access(const Thing& t) {
    // ...
    last_accessed_thing = &t;
}

extern Thing get_a_thing();
void f() {
    access(get_a_thing());
    // last_accessed_thing is dangling
}
```

The temporary `Thing` object that was returned by `get_a_thing` can be destroyed by the compiler at any time after `access` returns, which leaves the `last_accessed_thing` pointer dangling.

Mark Linton has suggested a programming convention that helps avoid this kind of bug:

> Functions should not store pointers to *reference* arguments in any location that will persist after the function returns. Functions that need to do this should use *pointer* arguments instead.

This convention makes sense. A call that passes a reference argument is written like a call that passes an argument by value; it is easy for programmers to lose track of the difference between the two cases. As we saw in Section 2.7.1, class designers take advantage of this by using const reference arguments for arguments that are conceptually passed by value—the use of const references is just a performance optimization. This practice makes it unlikely that programmers will remember cases where a const reference argument is "remembered" by the called function. In a similar vein, programmers tend to view *non*const reference arguments as arguments that will be actively changed during the function call. They are likely to be surprised if calling a function with a reference argument causes the object to change at some point after the function returns.

If `access` takes a `const Thing*`, the call looks very different:

```
extern void access(const Thing*); // Stores the pointer
extern Thing get_a_thing();

void f() {
    Thing t = get_a_thing();
    access(&t);
}
```

This version still leaves `last_accessed_thing` dangling, but a programmer trying to diagnose a crash caused by a dangling pointer is much more likely to be suspicious of this code.

The Linton convention is especially important when the fact that the function stores a pointer is not obvious from looking at the code. If that fact *is* obvious, you may want to violate the Linton convention if the resulting code would otherwise be too ugly. For instance, the constructor for our `Listiter` template from Chapter 8 takes a `List&` argument and stores a pointer to that `List` inside the `Listiter` being constructed. The creation of an iterator is a very common action, so it is important to make it as terse as possible. The use of a reference argument lets us write

```
List<int> iter(list);
```

instead of

```
List<int> iter(&list);
```

Since an iterator is an abstraction of a pointer into a container, the fact that the iterator "remembers" the container should not be a surprise to someone reading the code.

9.3   Memory management

Language designers are of two minds when it comes to memory management. Some think it is so important that it must be left to the programmer while others think it is so important that it must *not* be left to the programmer. C++ (like C) falls into the first category. This gives the programmer the most flexibility, but if you mess up, the consequences can range from harmless (and often unnoticed) memory leaks to programs that crash or simply do the wrong thing.

C++ contains mechanisms that can help class designers and users avoid memory problems. The help does not come automatically; you must ask for it, by designing your classes to reduce the chances of memory problems.

In this section, we present several schemes that help get the deletes right. The key idea is to let the computer keep track of the allocated memory in a way that frees the programmer from having to remember to do the delete.

9.3.1   Using constructors and destructors for memory management

The safest **new** appears in a constructor, with a corresponding **delete** in the destructor. The rules of C++ make sure[2] that automatic objects and globals are destroyed exactly once. The C-ish alternative of just remembering to delete the memory is bug prone. Consider this function, which builds

---

[2]Sort of. See Section 9.6 for some traps.

employee names with multiple spaces collapsed into a single space:

```
void
enter_employee(const char* name) {
    char* canon = new char[strlen(name)+1];
    char* cp = canon;
    char last = 'X';
    while (*name) {
        if (!(*name == ' ' && last == ' '))
            *cp++ = *name;
        last = *name++;
    }
    *cp = '\0';
    employee_database.enter(canon);
    delete[] canon;
}
```

This works, but it is a bug waiting to happen. It is easy for a later modification to inadvertently introduce a path that does not free the memory. For example, suppose that any name containing a @ represents an "off the books" employee, so the program is changed in the following way:

```
void
enter_employee(const char* name) {
    char* canon = new char[strlen(name)+1];
    char* cp = canon;
    char last = 'X'; // Any nonblank

    while (*name) {
        if (*name == '@')  // Off the books?  *CHANGE*
            return;        //                 *CHANGE*
        if (!(*name == ' ' && last == ' '))
            *cp++ = *name;
        last = *name++;
    }
    *cp = '\0';
    employee_data.enter(canon);
    delete[] canon;
}
```

The addition of the check for @ introduces a bug: memory will be lost whenever the **return** is taken.

Bugs like this are much less likely if the memory is maintained by an object with a destructor. Here is the preceding example, using a `String` class instead of `char*`s:

```
void
enter_employee(const String& name) {
    String canon;
    char last = 'X'; // Any nonblank
    int len = name.length();

    for(int i = 0; i < len; ++i) {
        char ch = name[i];
        if (ch == '@')  // Off the books?
            return;
        if (!(ch == ' ' && last == ' '))
            canon.append(ch);
        last = ch;
    }
    employee_data.enter(canon);
}
```

Here, the memory is maintained by the implementation of `String`. Whenever the flow of control leaves this function (either by a return or by a thrown exception), all of the existing automatic objects (in this case, `canon`) are properly destroyed, avoiding the memory leak.

9.4   Alternative memory allocation schemes

The use of an automatic object to handle memory deallocation works only when the memory is allocated and freed in the same function invocation. That is not always possible; in this section, we look at a couple of common schemes that work even when the allocation and deallocation occur in different functions.

9.4.1   Use counting using smart pointers

We have already covered one of the schemes in detail: pointers that manage use counts in objects and delete them when the use counts become zero were discussed in Chapter 7.

9.4.2   Garbage collection by logging all pointers and objects

An alternative to use counts involves keeping track of all existing (smart) pointers to objects and also keeping track of the pointed-to objects. Periodically, a "garbage collector" examines all existing pointers and marks every object that is pointed at. It then removes any pointed-to objects that are unmarked.

This approach has advantages and disadvantages. Changing the *value* of a garbage collected pointer is as fast as changing the value of a dumb pointer, while changing the value of a use-counted pointer involves fiddling with one or two use counts (see the code on page 154.) On the other side of the balance sheet, the creation and destruction of the pointers and the pointed-to objects is more expensive, since these operations must update the data structures that keep track of existing pointers and objects. The application designer must also decide when to run the garbage collection routine (with use counts, the collection is done on the fly—there is no separate garbage collect). For real-time systems, there may not be enough time to complete the garbage collect before a response to some other activity is required, which complicates the logic of the garbage collector.

Nevertheless, if pointers change their values frequently but the pointers and objects are not created and destroyed frequently, these schemes can give the best performance.

It is still true that otherwise unreachable objects in pointer cycles will not be collected. This can be dealt with by enhancing the garbage collector to know about *root* pointers. If it is true that all "live" objects are either pointed to by a root pointer, or by a pointer inside of another live object, then the garbage collector can start at the roots and follow all of the pointers, marking every pointed-to object. It is harder to build a general library that supports this kind of garbage collection, because the garbage collector must be able to find all of the pointers in an object. In practice, the most common approach is to handcraft a separate function for every class.

9.4.3   Arenas

Arenas are among the easiest memory management schemes to program, but they work only for certain kinds of applications. Each object is created "in" an arena. Later, the arena is emptied, which causes all of the objects in that arena to be deleted.

For example, imagine a C++ parser that parses a sequence of files, each of which contains a sequence of external declarations. As it parses, the parser might create a series of symbol tables that represent names declared at various points of the parse. The author of the parser might decide that the symbol table(s) for symbols declared inside of a function could be discarded when the parse of the function was complete; but the symbol table(s) for the symbols declared at file scope could not be discarded until a file was complete. These two different kinds of symbols would be allocated in two different arenas; the function-level arena would be emptied after every function, and the file-level arena would be emptied after every file.

The arena logic is independent of the objects stored in the arena, so we implement it as a template. An arena maintains a set of pointers to the objects in the arena:

```
template <class T>
class Arena {
private:
    Set<T*> contained;
public:
    Arena() {}
    ~Arena() { empty(); }

    void enter(T* p) { contained.insert(p); }
    void empty();
};
```

When an object wishes to identify itself as being in an **Arena**, it calls the **Arena**'s **enter** function, passing **this** as the argument. At any time, we can explicitly **empty** an **Arena**, which destroys all of the Ts "in" the arena:

```
template <class T>
void
Arena<T>::empty() {
    Setiter<T*> iter(contained);
    T* tp;
    while(iter.next(tp)) {
        contained.remove(tp);
        delete tp;
    }
}
```

To be safe, the **Arena** destructor also empties the arena.

Of course, since the objects are deleted by the arenas, objects using arenas must always be allocated with **new**, must not be entered into two or more arenas, and must not be deleted by anyone else (see question 6).

Using the operand of delete

There is a subtle programming trap in **Arena<T>::empty**: we must remove the pointer from the **contained** set before we delete it. According to the rules of C++, if the operand of a **delete** is a modifiable lvalue, its value is undefined after the delete. This rule was added to allow a compiler implementation to change the value of **tp** (usually by setting it to zero) after the delete, to make it more likely that bugs like this would be caught:

```
// ...
delete ptr;
return ptr->foo;
```

But this means that we must not depend on **tp** being meaningful after the delete. This is a bug:

```
template <class T>
void
Arena<T>::empty() {
    Setiter<T*> iter(contained);
    T* tp;
    while(iter.next(tp)) {
        delete tp;
        contained.remove(tp); //Bug!
    }
}
```

This code will work (by luck) on implementations where **delete** is nondestructive, but will break when ported to a C++ implementation that sets **tp** to zero after the delete.

class Symbol

We can now use our **Arena** template to store our compiler's symbol tables. One of the arguments to the **Symbol** constructor will be the **Arena<Symbol>** the new **Symbol** is in. (Note that it is "in" the arena only in the abstract sense; the **Symbol** is still physically stored on the heap.) Each **Symbol** will notify its arena when it is created:

```
class Symbol {
// details omitted...
public:
    Symbol(Arena<Symbol>&, const char*);
    ~Symbol();
};


Symbol::Symbol(Arena<Symbol>& arena, const char* d) {
// construct the Symbol, then ...
    arena.enter(this);
}
```

We have assumed that the arena for each Symbol is passed as a constructor argument; other schemes are possible (such as using a global or making the decision based on the contents of the Symbol).

9.5   Passing arguments to operator new

The arena a Symbol is in says nothing about where the Symbol is physically stored. Instead, the arena says something about the object's abstract behavior: it determines when the object will be destroyed. Like most other information that specifies behavior, the Arena is specified by an argument to the constructor.

If you want to control where, physically, the object will be stored, C++ allows you to pass arguments to the new operator (see the Review on the next page).   Since operator new just gets the memory—it does not initialize the object—its arguments should help it decide where the object will be physically stored; otherwise, those arguments should be passed to the constructor, not operator new.

A valid use of the placement syntax might involve an application running on a platform that had a limited amount of fast memory. When an object is newed, operator new can be passed an extra argument which will cause the object to be built in fast memory:

```
extern void* malloc_fast_memory(size_t); //get fast memory
enum Memory_kind { fast_mem, slow_mem };
```

Review: Placement syntax

A user can pass arguments to `operator new` by supplying them in a parenthesis-enclosed list immediately after the `new` keyword:

```
Memory_info info;
Thing* tp = new (info) Thing;
```

These arguments are passed as extra arguments to `operator new`, after the implicit first `size_t` argument (which specifies how many bytes to allocate). There must be an `operator new` (either class-specific or global) that can be called with those arguments. In our preceding example, there must be one that takes `size_t` as its first argument and `Memory_info` as its second argument:

```
void*
operator new(size_t bytes, Memory_info info) {
// details omitted
}
```

Some C++ implementations include (in `new.h`) a special `operator new` that can be used to specify the exact location of a new object:

```
void*
operator new(size_t, void* where) {
    return where;
}
```

This form can be used to force a new object to be constructed in a particular place:

```
#include <new.h>
main() {
/* Build a Thing at memory location 0x1234.*/
    new ((void*)0x1234) Thing;
```

This causes a `Thing` to be constructed at location 0x1234. Users of this function had better know what they are doing.

```
void*
operator new(size_t bytes, Memory_kind kind) {
    if (kind == fast_mem)
        return malloc_fast_memory(bytes);
    else
        return malloc(bytes);
}
```

Here is a call that asks for fast memory:

```
Thing* important = new (fast_mem) Thing;
```

9.5.1   Placement syntax and operator delete

While you can pass arguments to operator new, there is no way to pass
arguments to operator delete. If the delete operator needs to know something about how the memory was newed, it must figure it out based on the
value of its single void* argument. This is often done by maintaining a
separate data structure on the side:

```
static Set<void*> allocated_fast_memory;
```

```
void*
operator new(size_t bytes, Memory_kind kind) {
    void* vp;
    if (kind == fast_mem) {
        vp = malloc_fast_memory(bytes);
        allocated_fast_memory.insert(vp);
    }
    else {
        assert(kind == slow_mem);
        vp = malloc(bytes);
    }
    return vp;
}
```

```
void
operator delete(void* mem) {
    if (allocated_fast_memory.contains(mem)) {
        allocated_fast_memory.remove(mem);
        free_fast_memory(mem);
    }
    else
        free(mem);
}
```

Note that this does the right thing if the default `operator new` is used:

```
Thing* tp = new Thing; // no placement syntax
delete tp;
```

It would not be a bad idea to profile programs using this memory allocation scheme to make sure that the gains from the fast memory are not erased by the extra overhead of managing the `Set`.

Of course, if a pointer to fast memory can be detected by examining its value—perhaps all fast memory is in a known address range—then a side data structure is unnecessary; `operator delete` can figure out what to do by examining its `void*` argument.

9.6   Managing external resources

You may be tempted to use objects to control other resources, including resources that are not part of the running process. For instance, you might have an object that represents a lock on some portion of a database; when the object is destroyed, that lock will be freed. If you attempt this, keep in mind that there are various ways to end a process that do not call all of the destructors for existing automatic variables.

Under the current language rules, `exit()` causes static objects to be destroyed, but does *not* destroy the automatics! If you are depending on the destruction of an automatic to free some resource that is *outside the process*—such as a database lock—you will be in trouble. There may be other system calls that have the same problems. In UNIX System V and similar operating systems, a call to any of the `exec()` functions or to `abort()` will not cause automatics to be destroyed; and a call to `fork()` that is not followed by an `exec()` will cause the automatics to be bitwise duplicated, causing the external resource to be released twice!

9.7   Finding memory bugs

In spite of your best efforts, it is likely that sooner or later you will be faced with debugging code that has memory problems: either a memory leak, deleting memory more than once, or using memory that has already been deleted. This section will discuss some common techniques for detecting and fixing these bugs.

9.7.1   Senseless violence in destructors

Bugs involving use of memory that has already been deleted are particularly nasty, because such programs often—but not always—work, by luck. The bug shows up only when the memory allocator reallocates the memory while it is still being used. If the interval between the `delete` and the (invalid) subsequent use is small, the odds of the memory allocator reallocating the memory are small (but not zero!), making the bug hard to reproduce.

One way to catch these bugs is to have every destructor gratuitously scribble on the memory used by the object. A subsequent use of the object will be immediately caught, even if the memory allocator has not reallocated the memory. For example,

```
class Employee {
private:
    String   name;
    int      salary;
public:
    // details omitted
    ~Employee();
};


Employee::~Employee() {
    salary = -1; // Or some other obviously bad value
}
```

If there is a bug involving the use of a destroyed `Employee`, it should now show up immediately as an obvious and reproducible problem (such as an attempt to issue a check for `$-1`), rather than as an occasional and hard-to-reproduce crash.

In our example, when an `Employee` is destroyed, the `name` member will itself be destroyed by a call to the `String` destructor. If that destructor scribbles on its data, `Employee` does not have to worry about it; it needs only to scribble on the members that are not class objects with destructors.

If the run time cost of the scribbling is an issue, it can be conditionally compiled out:

```
Employee::~Employee() {
#ifndef NDEBUG
    salary = -1;
#endif
}
```

9.7.2 Instrumented new and delete

Another technique involves using a special version of `::operator new` that remembers each pointer it returns and a corresponding version of `::operator delete` that issues an error if its operand was not returned by `::operator new` (or was deleted more than once).

This is straightforward, but there is one snag: our implementation of `::operator new` cannot use any classes that themselves call `::operator new`. Since most useful container classes do so, we are reduced to writing C-ish code that uses `malloc` and `free`. Our `::operator new` will call `malloc` and store the result in an array of pointers before returning it. Most of the logic in this routine deals with growing the array of pointers when necessary:

```
#include <stdlib.h>
#include <assert.h>

/* For simplicity (this is just for debugging!) ignore
new_handler issues. */

static void** active_ptrs = 0; /* ''block'' of
                                    outstanding ptrs */
static int active_ptrs_l = 0; // size of active_ptrs
static int used_ptrs = 0; // Number of nonzero entries
const int chunk_size = 100;  // How fast to grow

extern void*
operator new(size_t size) {
    /* Get the memory that was asked for. */
    void* mem = malloc(size);
    assert(mem);
```

```
/* Remember the pointer. Can't use any objects that use
   operator new in their implementation! */

if (used_ptrs == active_ptrs_l) {
    /* Need to grow. */

    int new_size = active_ptrs_l + chunk_size;
    if(active_ptrs)
        active_ptrs = (void**)realloc(active_ptrs,
            new_size*sizeof(void*));
    else
        active_ptrs = (void**)malloc(
            new_size*sizeof(void*));
    assert(active_ptrs);

    /* Zero out the new entries */

    for(int i = active_ptrs_l; i <  new_size; ++i)
        active_ptrs[i] = 0;
    active_ptrs_l = new_size;
}

/* Find a place to store the pointer */

for(int i = 0; i < active_ptrs_l; ++i) {
    if (active_ptrs[i] == 0) {
        active_ptrs[i] = mem;
        ++used_ptrs;
        return mem;
    }
}
abort(); //Can't happen. Honest.
return 0;
}
```

Note the use of an abort() at the end of the function. It is good practice to put aborts in places that you think cannot be reached. If you are wrong, or some later change to the code makes it possible to reach that point, the abort will be triggered.

`::operator delete` will check to make sure that its argument was returned by `new`:

```
extern void
operator delete(void* v) {
    /* Delete of "0" is OK */
    if(!v)
        return;

    for(int i = 0; i < active_ptrs_l; ++i) {
        if (active_ptrs[i] == v) {
            active_ptrs[i] = 0;
            --used_ptrs;
            free(v);
            return;
        }
    }

    fprintf(stderr,
        "Delete of object that was not newed\n");
    abort();
}
```

A delete of 0 is explicitly legal (and harmless) under the rules of C++, so we must allow for that case.

The use of a linear search means that this memory allocator is slow, but it is going to be used only for debugging, so that is all right.

We can also use these routines to print information about current memory usage:

```
extern "C" void
print_allocated() {
    if (used_ptrs)
    {
        fprintf(stderr,"Allocated memory:");
        for(int i = 0; i < active_ptrs_l; ++i)
            if (active_ptrs[i])
                fprintf(stderr, "%#x\n", active_ptrs[i]);
    }
}
```

This function will print the address of each currently active block of memory. If we can arrange to call **print_allocated** on program exit (after the static objects have been destroyed) this routine can help us find memory leaks. The exact way to do this depends on your compiler and operating system. Notice that we have made this function **extern "C"**; this makes it callable from system routines that may be written in C or assembler.

We can use our instrumented **new** and **delete** to catch another common bug. Programs with this bug often work by luck, but they can break when used with user-supplied memory allocators or when ported to other compilers. For example:

```
class String {
    char*    rep;
public:
    String(const char* = "");
    ~String();
// details omitted
};
String::String(const char* cp)
: rep(new char[strlen(cp)+1]) {
    strcpy(rep,cp);
}
String::~String() {
    free(rep); //bug!
}
```

Every **new** must have a corresponding **delete**. This code has a **free** instead; it will work (by luck) as long as **::operator new** calls **malloc**. This is the default behavior on most C++ implementations; but this code will break if **::operator new** is replaced by any version that does not call **malloc**. (Remember that any user, not just the provider of **String**, can supply an **::operator new** at link time!) A call to **print_allocated** will find the bug, since memory that was not **deleted** will appear as a memory leak.

A similar bug can occur if a **malloc** has a corresponding **delete**; in this case our instrumented routines will catch the error when the **delete** is done.

9.7.3 Delete of an array

According to the rules of C++, whenever you delete an array, you must use the **delete []** syntax. The **[]** tells the compiler to generate code that figures out how large the array is, and calls the destructor on each element of the array. If the [] is not supplied, only the first element is destroyed.

If the array elements are built-in types, there is no destructor, so forgetting the [] works by luck on most (if not all) compilers:

```
void main() {
    char* cp = new char[2];
    delete cp;
};
```

Although this works by luck, the language rules state that the behavior of this program is undefined! Deleting an array has undefined behavior if the [] is missing, regardless of the element types. It is bad practice to write code that works by luck, so you should delete all arrays, regardless of the element types, with the delete [] syntax.

9.7.4   Take advantage of commercial leak checkers

Several products on the market do more aggressive checking of memory usage. If at all possible, take advantage of them; you can assume that any large C or C++ program that has not been checked for memory leaks contains memory leaks.

9.8   Name collisions

If two libraries used in the same program define the same global name, there will be a collision at link time:

```
// In file Buffer.c

void flush_all() {
// ... details omitted
}

//In file Toilet.c

void flush_all() {
// ... details omitted
}
```

If both functions are in files that define other symbols, the other symbols will (hopefully) force both files to be loaded, and the loader will complain about duplicate symbols being defined. If both functions are in files all by themselves, only one of the files will get loaded, and all calls to `flush_all()` will call that function.

C++ is still a big improvement over C in this regard: since the argument types of a normal (C++ linkage) function are part of its signature, these two names do not collide:

```
// In Buffer.h:
void handle(Buffer*);

// In Toilet.c:
void handle(Toilet*);
```

Although it is less likely than in C, there is no way to guarantee that two libraries will not have name collisions that make them unusable in the same program. Until some kind of module facility is added to C++, all you can do is design your classes to make name collisions less likely, by reducing your *pollution of the global name space*.

Here is one approach. The aim is to incorporate class names into external symbols, so that instead of having a collision when two libraries define the same external name, two libraries will collide only if they define the same *class* name.

1. Adopt the common convention of capitalizing type names, but not function and data names; this will avoid collisions between type names and nontype names.

2. Choose class names that are unlikely to collide with another library.

3. Make those names part of the signature of your global functions and data, using static members when necessary.

9.8.1 Classes

It is important to choose a class name that is unlikely to collide with another library. Avoid names like

- `Object` or derivatives like `Obj`;

- `Node`;

- `Info`;

- Unit.

If you build a hierarchy rooted at `Object`, no one will be able to use your classes with any other library that does the same thing.

Collisions are not an issue with nested classes, since the enclosing class is part of the nested class's name:

```
class Entity_network {
public:
    class Object {
        // details omitted
    };
};
```

`Entity_network::Object` will not collide with any other `Object` class.

9.8.2   Functions

As noted previously, functions whose argument lists include class types will not collide as long as the class names are unique:

```
class Telephone_number { /* ... */ };

void dial(const Telephone_number&);
```

`dial(const Telephone_number&)` will not collide with any other `dial` that takes different arguments.

Member functions are also not a problem, since the signature of a member function includes the name of its class:

```
class Telephone_number {
public:
    void dial();
};
```

`Telephone_number::dial()` will not collide with any other `dial` that is not a member of class `Telephone_number`.

Collisions are still possible for normal (nonmember) functions that take no arguments or just built-in types as arguments. Such functions can still be kept out of the global name space. If a function is not part of the interface to a library and all calls to the function are from a single file, then giving the function file static linkage is the best choice (just as it is in C). Otherwise, the best way to keep the function out of the global name space is to make it a *static member function* of some class. If you have global data and you cannot make it file static, you can keep it out of the global name space by making it a *static data member* of some class:

```
class Displayed_object {
private:
    static Set<Displayed_object> all_objects;
public:
    static void display_all_objects();
};
```

`all_objects` and `display_all_objects` are not in the global name space. Unless the reference is inside a member function (or nested class) of `Displayed_object`, the enclosing class name must be specified:

```
void refresh() {
    Displayed_object::display_all_objects();

}
```

Static members can be private; this can be used to prevent users from accessing nonmember functions and data that are part of your implementation.

Functions with C linkage

Functions with C linkage do not include the argument types in their signature. Such functions will collide with any other C linkage function with the same name, regardless of the argument types:

```
//Badly named C-linkage function
extern "C"
void write(int filedes, Telephone_number* tn) {
// ...
}
```

The author of this function was trying to make it callable from C; but this function will collide with the `write` function from the standard C library. When you give a C++ function C linkage, you make it callable from C, but you also make it possible for the function to collide with any other function that has C linkage (which includes all functions written in C!).

9.9   Performance

One reason for the success of C++ is "inherited" from C: C++ programs are fast. That does not mean that every C++ program is fast enough. Many techniques commonly used to make C programs faster, such as the judicious use of register variables or using pointers instead of array subscripting, will also work for C++. This is especially true if you are examining a critical section of code, with the goal of optimizing every single line to the utmost.

However, as programmers make better use of data abstraction (including the use of libraries), they end up programming at a higher level. This allows an individual to be responsible for much more functionality than was previously possible; but it also means that, with the exception of certain critical sections of code, it will no longer be cost effective for programmers to worry about line-by-line performance issues. Instead, programmers will have to look for optimizations on a higher level.

Before we get into ways to make your programs faster, here is a warning: correctness is more important than speed. Computer cycles continue to get cheaper relative to human cycles; a performance improvement that also makes the code much harder to understand and maintain should be viewed with suspicion.

9.10   Don't guess, measure!

Humans are notoriously bad at predicting the performance bottlenecks of a large program. This is especially true when using abstract data types, since hiding implementation details (one of the goals of data abstraction) also hides the potential performance bottlenecks. Even if the documentation of a class specifies its performance characteristics, the documentation might be wrong. So, you should *measure your performance* by using a profiler—don't guess. By measuring the performance, you will concentrate your effort on the critical bottlenecks, and avoid wasting your effort optimizing code that only accounts for one percent of the run time.

When you discover a performance bottleneck, your first task should be to convince yourself that it really is a performance issue and not a bug. If you are spending too much time in a certain constructor because a bug is causing you to create 10,000 too many objects, speeding up that constructor is *not* the right approach! Check the call counts in the profiler output, along with any other information—such as line-by-line execution counts—that you have available. Only if the numbers seem right—your program is doing what you thought it was doing—should you worry about optimizations.

9.11 Algorithms

The biggest performance problems—and the most dramatic performance improvements—come from the fundamental algorithms used by your application. Before you worry about register variables, step back and look at your algorithms, paying especially close attention to their complexity. An algorithm that has $O(n^3)$ complexity may not be a problem on small test cases, but may dominate the application when run in the field with an n that is 20 times larger.

As an example of a broken algorithm, suppose that our List class from Chapter 8 has an `operator[](int i)` function that gives access to the ith element of the List, so that `lst[0]` gives the 0th element of `lst`, `lst[1]` gives the next element, and so on. Suppose also that a user walks through a list like this:

```
for (int i = 0; i < lst.length(); ++i)
    look_at(lst[i]);
```

What is the complexity of this loop? It depends on the complexities of `List::length()` and `List::operator[]`. They ought to be documented; for the sake of this example, we assume that `length()` takes constant time. If it does not, or if the constant is not small, this loop should be rewritten to call `length()` just once:

```
List<Thing> lst;
int len = lst.length();
for (int i = 0; i < len; ++i)
    look_at(lst[i]);
```

Let's further assume that the run time of `operator[](i)` is proportional to i. (This would be true if the ith element were found by starting at the head of the list.) If `len` is the length of the list, then the complexity of our loop (which calls `operator[]` once for every element in the list) will be quadratic.

Once we have done this analysis, one fix is obvious: use list iterators to step through the list, since the operation of stepping from one element of the list to the next should be $O(1)$ (constant time). An alternative would be to enhance List to cache the result of the last call to `operator[]`, so that a subsequent call could start at the cached position. This would work, but any operation that changed the state of the List would have to make sure to flush the cache.

9.11.1   Documenting the performance complexity

Data abstraction is a double-edged sword when it comes to performance. When the implementation of a library is visible to its users, those users can usually tell which operations are cheap and which are expensive. If you do a good job of data abstraction, the implementation will be invisible to the users, so they probably will not have a good sense of the cost of a particular operation—unless you tell them. If you are a library provider, you should *document the performance complexity* of your routines, especially those that do not run in constant time. Your users will need this information to calculate the performance complexity of their own algorithms.

Yes, this makes an aspect of your implementation visible to your users; but there is no way to avoid this. The performance characteristics of a library will always be "visible" to its users, in the sense that users can tell how long their programs take to run. Documenting your performance characteristics just helps your users figure out the performance characteristics of their own algorithms.

Of course, when the complexity is documented, it becomes part of the contract between the library provider and the library user. A change that degrades the performance complexity of some function is almost as bad as an incompatible change to the signature of a member function, since it alters the complexity of user algorithms that call the function.

9.12   Bottlenecks in dynamic memory allocation

C++ programs tend to work the dynamic memory allocator a lot harder than C programs. Using dynamic memory in C is error prone and is therefore usually avoided whenever the programmer can get away with it; but using a C++ class object whose implementation uses dynamic memory allocation (like String) is easy, since the dynamic memory details are invisible to the user.

This means that the run time performance of the dynamic memory allocator (which we will refer to as malloc, although it can have different names on different systems) can dominate the run time performance of the entire program. This section discusses ways to tune the performance of programs that are spending too much time in `malloc`.

9.12.1   Understand how your application uses memory

Once you have convinced yourself that the problem is not a logic bug or a flawed algorithm, the next step is to understand how memory is being used. This might help you understand how to refine the design, or it might help you choose or design specially tuned memory allocators. Ask yourself questions like:

- Is the bulk of the memory used by a small number of classes? Which ones?

- Does your application allocate chunks of memory in a few fixed sizes, or does it allocate chunks of many different sizes?

- Does the application free memory as it runs, or docs it more or less continuously allocate memory, freeing it all at the end?

- Could a reasonable design change reduce the amount of memory that needs to be allocated? For instance, if a lot of the allocation cost is due to copying objects, an implementation that uses use counts and copy-on-write (see Chapter 7) might help.

9.12.2   Try several memory allocators

There are a variety of `malloc` implementations out there; some will work better for a given application than others. One `malloc` might work best with applications that rarely free memory; another might work best with applications that use chunks of a few distinct sizes; and a third might work best with applications that do random `new`s and `delete`s of varying sizes.

If `malloc` is a problem, start by building your application with every `malloc` (or other implementation of `::operator new`) you can get your hands on. Measure the performance of each version; you may be surprised at the differences. (I have seen an application that was spending 50 percent of its time in `malloc` reduce that percentage to less than five percent by switching to a different `malloc`.) It is a good idea to grow a local `malloc` collection; trying different `malloc`s is one of the easiest ways of speeding up your programs.

9.12.3   If needed, write your `operator new`

If all else fails, you may need to write your own **operator new**. The design of general purpose memory allocators is beyond the scope of this book. However, there is a common special case that we should address: memory allocated while constructing an object. Every time you say **new Thing;** you are, by default, calling **::operator new** to allocate **sizeof(Thing)** bytes of memory. This will work, but you may be able to specify a *class-specific* **operator new** that is much faster (see the Review opposite).   The global **new** operator must handle a request for any number of bytes, so it must use a general algorithm. However, if we ignore the possibility of derived classes for the moment, a class-specific **new** operator will only get requests for a single size: the size of the class. This makes it possible for the allocator to use a simpler and faster algorithm.

Providing a class-specific **operator new()** will not speed up the allocation of arrays, since these allocations do not use the class-specific **operator new()**. However, since the allocation of an array involves one call to **operator new** but many calls to the constructor (one per element), the run time overhead of the **new** is less likely to be a significant percentage of the time to create the array.

Class-specific `operator new` using `Pool`s

In this section, we show how the performance of a class can be significantly improved by using a class-specific **new** operator. We use the **Pool** class from the USL Standard Components library; but the approach should work with any fast memory allocator that deals with fixed-sized chunks of memory.

A **Pool** is an object that manages memory chunks of a single, fixed size (the size is an argument to the **Pool** constructor). Each call to **Pool::alloc()** returns a **void*** pointer to a new chunk of memory; that chunk can be returned to the **Pool** by calling **Pool::free**. The restriction on its functionality allows a **Pool** to use a much faster algorithm than a general purpose **malloc**; allocating memory often turns out to require just a few instructions executed inline.

We can use a **Pool** to speed up the allocation of a class **Thing** by creating a static **Pool** member of **Thing** that handles chunks of **sizeof(Thing)** bytes. **Thing** also declares class-specific **new** and **delete** operators:

Review: Class-specific new and delete

A class-specific new operator can be specified by declaring and defining a member function named operator new:

```
#include <stddef.h>
class Thing {
public:
    void* operator new(size_t);
    void operator delete(void*);
};
```

Like the global ::operator new, the first argument to a class-specific operator new must be a size_t (which is defined in stddef.h); the function must return a void* that points at the allocated memory. If there are any additional arguments, that operator new can be called only by using the placement syntax. A class-specific delete operator can also be declared as a member function; it takes a void* that points to the memory to be deleted.

These member functions will be used whenever an individual object of the class is newed and deleted. They are *not* used when arrays of objects are newed and deleted; the global ::operator new is used in that case.

A class-specific new or delete is inherited by any derived classes; the argument to new will reflect the correct size of the derived class:

```
class Derived_thing : public Thing {
private:
    int mem;
public:
    Derived_thing();
};
```

When a Derived_thing is newed, its memory will be allocated by a call to:

```
Thing::operator new(sizeof(Derived_thing));
```

```
// File Thing.h:
#include <Pool.h>
class Thing {
// details omitted
private:
    static Pool pool;
public:
    inline void* operator new(size_t);
    inline void  operator delete(void*);
};
```

The **new** operator calls **Pool::alloc** to get the memory for the **Thing**. (We explain the **assert** in Section 9.12.4.)

```
inline void*
Thing::operator new(size_t bytes) {
    assert(bytes == sizeof(Thing));
    return pool.alloc();
}
```

The **delete** operator returns the memory to the **Pool**:

```
inline void
Thing::operator delete(void* v) {
    pool.free(v);
}
```

Since the **Pool** is a static member, it must have a unique definition. The constructor argument specifies that the **Pool** manages chunks of **sizeof(Thing)** bytes:

```
// File Thing.c:
#include "Thing.h"
Pool Thing::pool(sizeof(Thing));
```

When a **Thing** is **new**ed, instead of a call to the default **operator new**, the compiler will call the (inline) class-specific version, which in turn calls **pool.alloc** (which is also inline) to get the memory for the **Thing**. The impact on performance can be significant, as we will see in the next section.

Adding Pools **to our** List **template**

Let's do some rudimentary performance analysis of the List template from Chapter 8. For a benchmark we will use a program that creates an empty List<int>, creates a Listiter<int> on that List, and uses the iterator to add 100 integers to the List. This is too simple to test the overall performance of the whole class, but it will at least give us an indication of the performance of list creation and insertion:

```
#include <iostream.h>
#include "List.h"
main() {
    for (int loop = 0; loop < 1000; ++loop) {
        List<int> intlist;
        Listiter<int> iter(intlist);
        for (int i = 0; i < 100; ++i)
            iter.insert_after(i);
    }
}
```

When run with optimizing on, we discover that this program spends about 21 percent of its time in malloc (on my system; your results may vary). This may seem surprising, since the user code does no news or deletes; but the List implementation does. In particular, adding an element to a List<T> causes a List_link<T> to be newed.

We can speed up the insert (and removal) operations by enhancing the List_link template to use Pools. We add the declarations of the Pool, and the class-specific new and delete, to the template declaration file:

```
// In List.h:
#include <stddef.h>
#include <Pool.h>

template <class T>
class List_link {
    static Pool pool;
public:
    inline void* operator new(size_t);
    void  operator delete(void* v) { pool.free(v); }
  // details omitted...
};
```

```
template <class T>
inline void*
List_link<T>::operator new(size_t size ) {
    assert(size == sizeof(List_link<T>));
    return pool.alloc();
}
```

We must also add the definition of `List_link<T>::pool` to the template definition file:

```
// In List.c:
template <class T>
Pool
List_link<T>::pool(sizeof(List_link<T>));
```

Always measure the effect of any performance improvement—if for no other reason than to make sure that the performance did not get worse! When I profiled our benchmark using this new version, the percentage of time spent in `malloc` dropped to around three percent, and the number of calls to `malloc` dropped from around 100000 to 1196.

9.12.4   The catch: derived classes

We paid a price for the improved performance of our `List` class. If anyone derives from `List_link` and adds data members (thereby changing the size of the class), the inherited `operator new` will not work properly, since its `Pool` handles chunks of the wrong size. Any derived class that changes the size must declare a new class-specific `operator new` that uses a `Pool` of the right size. Since `List_link` is a "private" class—users are not even aware of it—this is acceptable. If anyone but yourself is likely to derive from your classes, it becomes more of a judgment call: is the additional constraint on derived classes worth the extra performance?

In any case, just to be safe, it is a good idea to have an `operator new` that uses `Pools` check to make sure that the size of the object being created matches the size managed by the pool. That is what the `assert` in `List_link<T>::operator new` is for.

9.13   Inlines

Inline expansion is one of the most powerful performance tools provided by C++. For short functions, the expansion of the function may be shorter than the code for the calling sequence—in which case, the inline expansion is clearly a win. For almost all nontrivial functions, it is not so clear. In these cases, inline expansion is a tradeoff: the program gets larger (an extra copy of the code is expanded inline) but faster (no function call overhead).

When deciding whether to inline a function, the key idea is that *for inlining to be a win, the function call overhead should be a significant percentage of the time required to execute the function.* If the function call overhead is only 5 percent of the typical run time of the function, the savings will only be 5 percent of the time the entire application spends in that function. That is unlikely to be significant and may not even be measurable.

This implies that inline functions should be short: a few lines at most. A larger function will save a small percentage of its run time and will have a higher space penalty. Functions with loops should almost never be inlined. The run time of a loop that iterates more than once is likely to swamp the function call overhead; and many compilers do not inline functions with loops anyway (see Section 9.13.2).

9.13.1   Inlines calling inlines

Even if you inline only one-line functions, you can still make some pretty big functions. A one-liner may call two or three functions that are also inline; each of those functions may in turn call two or three inline functions, and so on.

Consider these apparently reasonable inline functions:

```
class Telephone_number {
public:
// details omitted
    String area_code() { /* ... */ }
    String exchange() { /* ... */ }
    String number() { /* ... */ }
    String formatted() { return "(" + area_code()
                + ") " + exchange() + "-" + number(); }
};
```

How big do you think `Telephone_number::formatted` is? In addition to calls to `area_code`, `exchange`, and `number`, there are also five calls to `operator+(String, String)`. Any or all of these calls may be inline. But that is not all—four `String`s to hold intermediate results are also created and destroyed. On my system, where the only inline functions are the three members of `Telephone_number` plus string construction and assignment, each call to `formatted` generates 552 bytes of code! This was large enough that the compiler simply refused to inline it—see the next section. Consider what would have happened if `String::operator+` was inline, too! This is one reason why C++ programs sometimes turn out to be larger than expected.

9.13.2   Outlined inlines

The `inline` directive is just a request; the compiler may decide not to honor the request for any particular call to an inline function. The function may be too large or complicated; or it may be impossible to fully inline because it is recursive. In this case, the compiler must lay down a noninline version of the function and generate a regular function call.

Many compiler implementations will lay down a file static copy of the function in the compilation unit containing the call. (This static copy is called an *outlined inline*.) If you declare an inline function that, due to its size, will *never* be inlined, you will get an outlined inline in each compilation unit that contains a call of the function.

The effect of this can be dramatic. I was once working on a program that had about 30 source files. I was concerned about performance, so I made lots of functions inline. Once I got an early version working, I was unpleasantly surprised by its size. I discovered that each of the 30 files contained 20K bytes of outlined inlines. That 600K bytes of text was about half of the text space of the entire program!

There are several ways to detect when you have outlined inlines. Your compiler may have a flag that will cause it to print a warning when it outlines an inline. An alternative is to run a tool like `nm` on your object files and look at the file static functions defined in each file. The details vary from system to system (and from compiler to compiler), but the outlined inlines are usually easy to spot.

Once you have diagnosed the presence of outlined inlines, the fix is easy: just make the offending functions noninline and recompile everything from scratch.

9.14   Tiemann's law

Finally, all library developers should remember Tiemann's Law:

> *"It isn't reusable if it hasn't been reused."*—Michael Tiemann

No library should be considered reusable if it has not been tried by someone other than its developer. This is the best way to discover any assumptions that the developer made (perhaps unconsciously) about how the library would be used. The new user(s) may also discover any missing functionality, missing, misleading or incorrect documentation, or other dependencies (such as dependence on a particular compiler).

Tiemann's law also leads to a corollary (attribution unknown):

"It isn't reusable if it isn't usable."

9.15   In short

- A prospective user should be able to decide whether a library is useful by looking at the first line of the manual page.

- Class names are the most important part of your documentation. Choose them carefully, and solicit the opinions of others to make sure the names make sense to someone other than yourself.

- Use frequent assertions to stop insane programs quickly.

- Avoid fixed-sized arrays, unless you know the array will *never* be too small.

- Provide debugging versions of libraries.

- Avoid class names (like `Object`) that have a high chance of clashing with other libraries.

- Use static members to avoid pollution of the global name space.

- Use objects to manage memory; don't do it by hand.

- Be aware that processes can go away without destroying all automatics.

- Delete all arrays using `delete []`, even if the elements have no destructor.

- Use tools to find memory leaks: write an instrumented `malloc` and `free`, or use a commercial product.

- To catch uses of already-destroyed objects, destructors should give their data members obviously invalid values.

- Correctness is more important than speed.

- Measure performance, don't guess!

- Document the complexity of library routines, especially those that do not run in constant time.

- Algorithmic improvements will usually have the greatest effect.

- Make sure a performance problem is not really the manifestation of a bug.

- Use a class like `Pools` to build fast class-specific memory allocators.

- Remember Tiemann's Law.

9.16   Questions

1. Why should you care if someone is too lazy to read your entire manual page to determine if your class is reusable?

2. What assumption does this code make about the size of the input? Is this reasonable?

   ```
   extern istream& operator>>(istream&, Employee&);
   int
   total_employee_salary(istream& in) {
        int total = 0;
        Employee emp;
        while(in >> emp)
                total += emp.salary();
        return total;
   }
   ```

3. We claimed that an `assert` is free when `NDEBUG` is turned on. But if the assert is the body of a conditional:

   ```
   if (kid)
        assert(kid->parent() == me);
   ```

   don't we still pay the cost for the test of the conditional even if `NDEBUG` is defined? If not, why not?

4. A collection of classes can be "packaged" by nesting them inside another class whose only purpose is to keep the names of its members outside of the global name space:

```
class Telephone_project {
public:
    class Telephone_number { /* ... */ };
    class Telephone { /* ... */ };
    class Switch { /* ... */ };
    // No nonstatic data members
    // No nonstatic member functions
};
```

Discuss the pros and cons of this approach. (Hint: how much typing is involved?) Should `Telephone_project` have any private members?

5. Our `Arena` template has the property that the contents of the `Arena` will be destroyed in a random order (since they are stored in an unordered `Set`). Change this class so that the contents of an `Arena` are destroyed in the reverse of the order in which they were entered into the `Arena`.

6. What happens if a user explicitly deletes a `Symbol` before clearing the arena it is in? How would you enhance the `Arena` template to support explicit deletion of elements in the `Arena`? (Hint: the hard part is making sure that nothing gets deleted twice.)

7. A class-specific `new` that uses `Pools` might try just calling the global `new` if the size does not match the `Pool`:

```
template <class T>
inline void*
List_link<T>::operator new(size_t size ) {
    if(size == sizeof(List_link<T>))
        return pool.alloc();
    return ::operator new(size);
}
```

But that is not enough. Why? (Hint: how does this affect `operator delete`?) Design an `operator delete` that will work with this `new`, and decide whether the additional processing and complexity is worth it.

8. Our `operator delete` on page 228 uses `stdio` instead of iostreams, as does the `print_allocated` function. Why?

9. Enhance `print_allocated` (and the `new` and `delete` operators if necessary) to print the size of each currently allocated memory block.

10. How might one use `Pools` in the implementation of a global `operator new`? (Thanks to Andrew Koenig for this idea.)

11. Does Tiemann's Law indicate a failure of the development process? Would a better process allow us to "do it right the first time" by designing a library that was reusable from the start? How might such a process work?

Chapter 10

Exceptions

In programs, as in life, things sometimes go wrong. The *exceptions* feature (see the Review, next page) allows programs to deal with unanticipated situations without forcing the programmer to explicitly check for these situations at every step of the code. In this chapter, we discuss where exceptions should be used in a design—and where they should be avoided.

10.1   A disclaimer

We will be looking at the basics of exceptions, but the reader is cautioned that exceptions are a new feature, and the ways they are used will undoubtedly evolve over the next several years. In particular, at the time this chapter is being written (December 1992), compilers that support exceptions are just beginning to appear. All developers are advised to keep abreast of the continuing developments in this area.

10.2   Why exceptions?

Why have a special language feature for exceptions? Traditionally, C programmers have had four ways of dealing with exceptional conditions:

- **Ignore them**—if something goes wrong, *que será, será*. This may in fact be the right thing to do for a quick-and-dirty tool that will be used only by a small group of people. However, this makes it hard to build something of product quality.

Review: Exceptions

The `throw` keyword is used to raise an exception. It takes a single operand of any type:

```
class Xcpt {
    // details omitted
public:
    Xcpt(const char*);
    const char* diagnostic();
};

void
allocate_resource() {
    if (allocation() == FAIL)
        throw Xcpt("Allocation fails!");
}
```

When the `throw` is executed, control will be passed up to the nearest enclosing *exception handler* that can deal with ("catch") the exception. A copy of the operand (in this case, an `Xcpt`) is passed to the exception handler.

Exception handlers are specified like this:

```
void
allocate_and_report_results() {
    try {
        allocate_resource();
    }
    catch (Xcpt& caught_Xcpt) {
        cout << caught_Xcpt.diagnostic() << "\n";
    }
}
```

The code in the braces after the `try` is a *try block*; the code in the braces after the `catch` is an exception handler.

Unless an exception is thrown, when the flow of control reaches the end of the try block, the exception handler(s) will be skipped and the program will continue after the handlers. When an exception is thrown, the run time system will begin to unwind the stack (calling destructors when appropriate), looking for a try block. When a try block is found, the type of the exception object (operand of the `throw`) is compared with each associated `catch`, in order. If the thrown object "matches" the type specified by a `catch`, control is transferred to that handler. When that handler is complete, control is transferred to the first statement after the handlers.

The thrown object "matches" if it is the same type as the caught type, it is derived from the caught type, or the thrown object is a pointer to a derived class and the caught type is a pointer to a base class. Implicit type conversions are *not* applied.

If none of the catch clauses is a "match," the run time system will continue to unwind the stack, looking for a catch that does "match." If there is no such catch clause, the function `terminate()` is called, which (by default) will abort the program.

A function can arrange to catch *any* exception like this:

```
main() {
    try {
        // The whole program goes here
    }
    catch (...) {
        //all otherwise uncaught exceptions caught here
    }
}
```

A `throw` without an operand rethrows the current exception:

```
try {
    // something
}
catch (Xcpt& ex) {
    if (can_handle(ex))
        handle(ex);
    else
        throw; //equivalent to "throw ex"
}
```

- **Abort**—detect exceptions, but provide no recovery mechanism. This is certainly preferable to undefined behavior when something goes wrong; but it may be unacceptable for a wide variety of applications. For instance, a program that acquires resources (such as a lock on a database) cannot be allowed to simply abort without releasing those resources.

- **Set a global error code or have functions return error codes**— these can be made to work, but careful programs end up spending a significant amount of processing time checking error codes. Forgetting to check the codes is a common source of bugs.

- **Use `setjmp` and `longjmp`**—when an exception is found, C programmers can use the `longjmp` function to transfer control to some recovery action.

There are several reasons why these schemes are not adequate for C++. First, in many circumstances, there is no return value to check. In particular, what do you do when something goes wrong in a constructor? Without exceptions, the only alternatives are to abort, or to create an object that is in some kind of error state and hope that the user of the object checks to see whether the creation succeeded.

C++ programs should not use `setjmp` and `longjmp`. This is because a `longjmp` will unwind the stack, *without destroying the automatic objects on the stack.* Having objects "go away" without having their destructors called is an invitation to chaos.

Exceptions provide a good answer to these problems; they also let programmers write their code without having to worry about errors at every function call.

10.3   An example exception

On page 210, we defined a function named `check` that took an integer argument and printed an error message if that argument was zero:

```
inline void
check(int expr, const String& diag) {
    if (expr == 0) {
        cerr << "Internal error: " << diag << endl;
        abort(); // Or throw exception
    }
}
```

We used this function instead of **assert** for checks that should always be performed, even if **NDEBUG** is not defined. Let's rewrite this function to throw an exception when the check fails. The thrown object will contain the diagnostic message:

```
class Check_failure {
private:
    String diagnostic_d;
public:
    Check_failure(const String& s) : diagnostic_d(s) {}
    String diagnostic() const { return diagnostic_d; }
};
```

The check function will throw a Check_failure object instead of aborting

```
inline void
check(int expr, const String& s) {
    if (expr == 0)
        throw Check_failure(s);
}
```

The call to check does not change:

```
void
f() {
    char* space = new char[BUFFSIZE];
    check(space != 0, "Memory allocation");
    // ...
}
```

If space is 0, check will throw a Check_failure object which can be caught by any function that declares an appropriate exception handler:

```
main() {
    try {
    // ... the whole program
    }
    catch (Check_failure diag) {
        cerr << "Internal error: " << diag.diagnostic()
        << endl;
        return 1;
    }
    return 0;
}
```

Control will be passed to the exception handler, and any automatic objects that were popped off of the stack will have been properly destroyed.

10.4   Exceptions should be exceptional

Now that we have seen an example of the proper use of an exception, let's discuss how they should *not* be used. Exceptions should be used only to handle exceptional conditions; they should not be used for normal flow of control in a program. For example, an exception should not be used to signal when you have reached the end of a list:

```
void process(const Thing&);

void
process_each(List<Thing>& list) {
    try {
        for(;;) {
            Thing t = list.get();
            process(t);
        }
    }
    catch (List::empty) {
    }
}
```

This code depends on the fact that the List class will throw an exception when a get is done to fetch an element from an empty List. This will give the right answer, but it is bad for several reasons.

- The flow of control is not obvious. (How would you feel if you were asked to maintain code that routinely used longjmp to exit from loops?) Anyone who reads the program has to understand that control will normally pass from somewhere in List::get to the catch phrase. Why use an advanced facility like exceptions when returning a value will work just as well?

```
void process(const Thing&);

void
process_each(List<Thing>& list) {
    Thing t;
    while(list.get(t))
            process(t);
}
```

This version is both shorter and simpler.

- When the stack is unwound following a thrown exception, any automatics on the stack will be destroyed. This does not guarantee that all resources will be freed. For example,

```
char* temp_stuff = new char[100];
use_stuff(temp_stuff);
delete [] temp_stuff;
```

If an exception is thrown inside of use_stuff and is caught in an outer scope, we have a memory leak, since the delete will never be executed. If the exception is an unusual case, this will probably be OK in practice. If this happens as part of the normal course of events (say, in a loop that executes thousands of times), the memory leak will be significant.

You can protect against this by following every new with a try block that catches any exception, deletes the memory that was newed, and then rethrows the exception:

```
char* temp_stuff = new char[100];
try {
    use_stuff(temp_stuff);
}
catch(...) {
    delete [] temp_stuff;
    throw;
}
delete [] temp_stuff;
```

But this is ugly, hard to get right, and even harder to test. A better approach would to use an automatic object to manage the resource (as we did with memory in Section 9.3.1); but even if you do this, it is unlikely that all of the libraries you are using will do it too.

- Unless you are careful, an exception used for normal flow of control can mask an exception raised due to an exceptional occurrence. Looking back at our loop on page 254, suppose that `process(const Thing&)` uses a temporary `List` and contains a logic bug that manifests itself as a `get` of that `List` when it is empty? In that case, control will silently be passed out of `process` to the exception handler in `process_each`, which will not realize that this is not the "normal" exception![1]

- There are several different schemes for implementing exceptions, with different run time characteristics. Exceptions will almost always be slower than normal straight-line code. Even if you happen to have a fast implementation of exceptions on your system, a subsequent port of your code to another architecture may cause a performance hit if that architecture uses a slow implementation.

10.5   Understanding exceptions

Given that we will reserve exceptions for exceptional cases, how do we use the things? When you think about a particular exceptional condition, ask yourself two questions:

1. Who or what is the source of the problem?

---

[1]It is no coincidence that *normal exception* is an oxymoron.

2. Who or what is going to deal with it? Will that party attempt to analyze the error? In particular, will the program attempt to recover from the error or will it simply exit more or less gracefully with a diagnostic message?

The answer to the first question often determines the answer to the second.

10.6   Blame assessment

First, figure out who or what caused the problem. The most likely candidates are the following:

10.6.1   You

This is the case when your program detects an internal logic error (such as an assertion failure). Other examples are "can't happen" cases, such as discovering a null pointer where one should not exist.

Most programs will not attempt to analyze internal logic errors. They will probably generate a human-readable diagnostic (e.g., "Internal error number 234; contact support organization") and either abort or perform some high-level recovery action.

10.6.2   Another programmer

If you are a library provider, you will often need to have some constraints on the inputs to your functions. The responsibility of meeting these *preconditions* rests with the programmer using your libraries. If a function is called and the preconditions are violated, raising an exception is appropriate. Examples would include an attempt to get the fifth character of a three character String or passing a null (zero) pointer to a function that did not expect it.

Again, it is unlikely that the user's program will want to analyze this error. The error message needs to be understandable by another programmer, but most programs will not care about the difference between these first two cases.

10.6.3   The provider of a resource

Some problems are not logic errors, but a failure to get some resource at run time. These errors might include running out of memory, a failure to acquire a database lock, a write failure due to a full disk, a timeout on a system call, or a failure to get some other resource (such as licenses from a license server).

These are the errors that a program would most likely be able to recover from. For instance, a program that runs out of memory might have some way of scrounging around to find some more. A failure to get a database lock might be handled by sleeping for some amount of time and trying again; a failure to get a license from a license server might be handled by displaying a diagnostic and offering the user the choice of waiting for a license to become free, aborting, or ordering new licenses ("enter your American Express card number:").

10.6.4   The user

These errors indicate a mistake by the user. These might include violating some constraint on input (e.g., entering alpha characters when a number was required) or requesting an inappropriate operation (writing a file that was edited with the readonly flag set).

Consider not using exceptions for user errors. Exceptions are most useful when the code that will deal with a problem is not the code that discovered it. However, the code that discovers a user error is often the code that can best deal with it. Also, exceptions are useful when you want to catch an error from any one of a sequence of operations and handle the error in the same way. But users need more coddling than programmers, and you may want to handle every user error individually. If you are giving every user error special treatment, the good old-fashioned method of checking the results of every operation may be the right approach.

Of course, there are no absolutes in computer science. Users may specify file names in many places in your programs, and you may want to catch every bad file name at the top level like this:

```
main() {
    try {
        // The whole program
    }
    catch (Bad_file_name n) {
        cerr << "Bad file name : " << n << endl;
    }
}
```

But this is unlikely to be good enough for a serious commercial product.

10.7   Designing the exception object

The exception object should be designed with an understanding of who (or what) is likely to analyze the exception. If a human will be analyzing the exception, the exception object will essentially be a string. The program usually just cares that the exception happened; it does not care about the details of the problem (other than a diagnostic to pass on to the human). If a program will be analyzing the exception, the exception object may be more complicated, since it will contain whatever data the program will need for its analysis.

For example, should a math library provide separate exceptions for division by zero and overflow?

```
// Overly complicated exception structure:
class Divide_by_zero_error {
// ...
};
class Overflow_error {
// ...
};

try {
    call_math_function(x,y);
}
catch (Divide_by_zero_error) {
    // ...
}
catch (Overflow_error) {
    // ...
}
```

Other than figuring out which diagnostic to print, it is hard to imagine a *program* that does different things for overflow and division by zero errors. Most programs will need to be notified only that the error happened, so they can print a diagnostic to the user and exit (or recover in some other way);

so a single exception class can be used to handle both cases:

```
class Math_error {
// ...
public:
    String diagnostic();
};

// ...

try {
    call_math_function(x,y);
}
catch (Math_error e) {
    cerr << "Math error:" << e.diagnostic() << endl;
}
```

But, you may ask, why not provide the different exceptions anyway, for those few programs that do care? What does it cost? Every exception, like every other feature, adds complexity to the package, and that complexity imposes a cost. The exceptions must be documented, which makes it that much harder to find the important parts of the class. Every user of the package must understand the exceptions, even if it is just to the point of deciding they can be safely ignored.

Remember the discussion in Chapter 1: if unsure, err on the side of making the interface too small. An error of omission can probably be repaired by adding a new exception class; but if you start out by providing a slew of different exception classes, you will be stuck documenting and maintaining them even if they are almost never used.

10.7.1   Exceptions and inheritance

When you design your exception objects, consider the use of inheritance to encapsulate concepts which are common to two or more classes. For instance, we might want to have an abstract base class `Diagnostic` for every exception that contained a human-readable string:

```
class Diagnostic {
public:
    virtual String diagnostic() = 0;
    virtual ~Diagnostic() {}
};
```

Our Check_failure and Math_error objects are consistent with this abstraction, so they could be derived from Diagnostic:

```
class Check_failure : public Diagnostic {
private:
    String diagnostic_d;
public:
    Check_failure(const String& s) : diagnostic_d(s) {}
    virtual String diagnostic() { return diagnostic_d; }
};


class Math_error : public Diagnostic {
// details omitted
};
```

The caller can arrange to catch *any* object that is derived from Diagnostic by including a handler that catches a Diagnostic&:

```
main() {
    try {
    // ... the whole program
    }
    catch (Diagnostic& diag) {
        cerr << "Internal error: " << diag.diagnostic()
        << endl;
        return 1;
    }
    return 0;
}
```

Note that the caller should catch a *reference* to the base class. Catches work just like function argument initialization; if the catch specified Diagnostic, only the Diagnostic part of the object would be caught (the object would be "sliced").

A reasonable refinement of our hierarchy might be to specify a new class Src_diagnostic, which is a Diagnostic that also includes source and line number information:

```
class Src_diagnostic : public Diagnostic {
public:
    virtual String source() = 0;
    virtual int line_number() = 0;
};
```

This is an exception that might be analyzed by both humans and programs. When a `Src_diagnostic` is thrown, a programming environment might use `source` and `line_number` to bring up a window centered on the specified line. On the other hand, since a `Src_diagnostic` *is-a* `Diagnostic`, a `catch` of a `Diagnostic&` will successfully catch a thrown `Src_diagnostic` and print its diagnostic string. (See also questions 4 and 5.)

Avoid `Exception`

Do not name any of your classes `Exception`. It is a name (like `Object`) that carries a high risk of name collision: it is not unlikely that other libraries will define classes with the same name. The risk is made even higher by the fact that the ISO/ANSI C++ standards committee is considering the creation of a "standard" `Exception` class.

10.8   In short

- Exceptions are a new feature and subject to change; follow the international standards effort closely in this area.

- Do not use exceptions for "normal" flow of control.

- Design your exception classes with an understanding of whether the exception will be analyzed by a human or by a program.

- Use inheritance where appropriate in the design of your exception classes.

- Do not name any class `Exception`.

10.9   Questions

1. Under what circumstances can a program that incorporates both C and C++ code use `setjmp` and `longjmp`?

2. Ada defines the following standard exceptions:

   - Constraint error—some operation violated an input constraint (such as an array index out of bounds).

   - Numeric error—a numeric operation produced an out-of-bounds result (e.g., overflow or underflow).

   - Program error—a program logic error (bug) has been detected.

   - Storage error—a request to get more memory failed.

   - Tasking error—an error occurred in the communications between two tasks.

   - Time error—a time limit for some operation was reached (time-out).

   - I/O exception—actually a family of exceptions, these specify that various input or output operations have failed.

   For each of these exceptions, assess the blame, identify whether the problem is likely to be dealt with by humans or programs, and state how you would handle such exceptions in C++.

3. Write an **Array** class that throws an exception when an out-of-bounds reference occurs. What type of object should be thrown?

4. Consider these alternative implementations for the **Diagnostic** and **Src_diagnostic** classes.

   ```
   class Diagnostic {
   private:
       String diagnostic_d;
   public:
       Diagnostic(const String& s) : diagnostic_d(s) {}
       String diagnostic() const { return diagnostic_d;}
       virtual ~Diagnostic() {}
   };
   ```

```
class Src_diagnostic : public Diagnostic {
private:
    String source_d;
    int    line_number_d;
public:
    Src_diagnostic(const String& diag,
    const String& src, int line)
    : Diagnostic(diag), source_d(src),
      line_number_d(line) {}
    String source() const { return source_d; }
    int line_number() const { return line_number_d; }
};
```

Compare these versions to the originals: what are the tradeoffs?

5. Enhance Src_diagnostic so that the value returned by the inherited diagnostic() member function will include the source file and line number.

Chapter 11

Moving your project to C++

Moving a project to C++ involves more than just some changes to the source code. The move involves training, a transition period, new design paradigms, new tools, and new procedures. A complete discussion of the program development process and how it is affected by C++ and object-oriented programming is beyond the scope of this book; nonetheless, we will attempt in this chapter to touch on some issues that seem to crop up more often than others.

This is not a chapter on "how to manage a C++ project." Instead, we are trying to give all of the participants of a multiperson project—not just the boss—an inkling of what to expect as the members of the project start building real C++ programs.

11.1 Choosing C++

One of the most important decisions is making the commitment to use C++ in the first place. The widespread availability of C++ compilers, tools, libraries, and environments makes the decision to choose C++ easier than it used to be; but there are risks as well as benefits.

11.1.1 Learning curve

The most obvious drawback is the learning curve. There really are two different learning curves when moving to C++: learning about the syntax and semantics of the language, and learning how to do object-oriented design.

C++ has a lot of features, but you do not need command of all of them to use the language effectively. For instance, most programmers I have talked to have never used pointers to members. That is not to say that the feature is not useful, only that the need for it arises in a limited set of applications. (That is why pointers to members are not covered in this book.) Most experienced C programmers seem to be able to learn the basics— classes, member functions, single inheritance, and so forth—in a week or so. That does not make them C++ experts; but they have enough command of the language to produce useful output in C++ while continuing their C++ education.

Learning object-oriented design takes more time. It is a fundamental mind shift that seems to take from three to six months for experienced C designers. This does not mean that the developers are not producing useful output in the meantime, or even that the first object-oriented design is worthless; instead, that is how long it usually takes until the designers describe themselves as comfortable with object-oriented design.

The timetable for the project must include an allowance for the learning curve. There is no hard-and-fast rule for calculating that allowance; but one data point is supplied by Jossman *et al*[1], who estimate that their project was "in the black" after a year: the productivity benefits of C++ more than paid for the learning curve costs in that time frame. On the other hand, a C project that faces an impossible three-month deadline will not be helped by turning to C++ in desperation.

11.1.2   Language and tools maturity

C++ has reached the stage where further language enhancements should be few and far between. There is widespread understanding that the language is already very large, and adding extra features to it would make it that much harder to master. In addition, the constraint of compatibility with the huge base of existing code makes further enhancements harder. The ISO/ANSI C++ standards committee expects to publish an official C++ standard in the mid-1990s. The major commercial C++ vendors have all agreed to follow the standard when it is completed.

Tools, libraries, and environments are not as mature. Each year sees the introduction of many new C++ development products. Object-oriented de-

---

[1]Jossman, P., Schiebel, E., and Shank, J., "Climbing the C++ Learning Curve," *Proceedings 1990 USENIX C++ Conference.*

sign tools that fully integrate the design and implementation phases (rather than just support the creation of design documents) are just beginning to appear.

11.1.3   Application constraints

> *"C++ isn't the best Smalltalk; Smalltalk is the best Smalltalk."*—
> Bjarne Stroustrup

C++ is an excellent general purpose language; that does not mean it is the best choice for every application. LISP may still be the right choice for AI; Smalltalk may be more appropriate for systems where flexibility and dynamic update are more important than run time performance and static type checking; programmers building small applications where performance is unimportant might be better off using AWK or Perl. C++ has a lot going for it, including the fact that it has a lot of suppliers competing for your business, but that does not mean that all other languages should be ignored.

11.2   Adopting C++

There are two schools of thought on how a development organization should go about learning C++. One school holds that programmers are lazy, and will not learn object-oriented design and other more advanced features of C++ unless they are pushed into it. This school advocates that a new C++ project ought to do it right the first time: begin by designing an object-oriented framework and attempt to do everything using objects from day one.

Having watched projects adopt C++ for several years, I have become a follower of the other school, which advocates that projects should "ease in" to C++ by adopting it in three phases:

- A better C;

- Data abstraction;

- Object-oriented programming.

11.2.1   C++ as a better C

In the first stage, the new C++ features are used as simple extensions to C. The fundamental designs and paradigms do not change; but features such as function argument typechecking, function overloading, inline functions, and `const` are used. Existing classes such as `String` can also be used. The benefit of this stage is that an entire project of C programmers with varying skills and experience can be doing useful work in C++ in a matter of days.

11.2.2   Data abstraction

The next step is to design and implement classes, with the emphasis on the separation of interface and implementation. These classes will often encapsulate the fundamental concepts of the application domain and are usually first designed and implemented by the more experienced and skilled members of the team. The use of inheritance and virtual functions is often limited.

11.2.3   Object-oriented programming

The final phase is the adoption of object-oriented designs. Inheritance and virtual functions become integral parts of the project. Since it is hard to alter an existing design to make it object-oriented, the first object-oriented design is usually either a new module or a reimplementation of an existing module.

11.2.4   Three steps vs. one step

Critics of the three step approach point out that programmers, and even entire projects, can get stuck at one of the earlier phases. That has not been the experience on projects that I have seen. The utility of data abstraction and object-oriented programming becomes obvious once the team members begin to experiment with them.

The second criticism is that the first C++ designs will have been done in the C paradigm, while they would have been better if they had been object-oriented. This must be weighed against the fact that the designs would have been done by people who were beginners in both C++ and object-oriented design. There is a lot of stuff in C++; asking the staff to bite it off all at once increases the risk that the entire project will be a failure. Object oriented design is a fundamental mind shift. It is a risky proposition to ask all of the members of a 40-person project, with varying levels of experience and expertise, to make this mind shift simultaneously.

11.3   Design and implementation

In this section, we talk about some of the things to expect as the project moves from doing preliminary designs into the detailed design and implementation phases.

11.3.1   C++ front loads the design process

C++ encourages designers to spend more time fully understanding the design before writing code. This is a benefit, as mistakes in the design are cheaper to fix when caught early; but it also means that significant time may pass before the first line of code is written.

11.3.2   Expect iteration

Software design is an iterative process. The first time around, an initial design is created, some initial classes are created, and a few high-level functions are implemented. At this point, the class designers will usually realize that the initial class design was flawed in some important way. The experience of *using* the classes points out where the understanding of the designers was incomplete. This does not necessarily indicate that the designers did not think hard enough before hacking code. It is difficult to anticipate all the issues and their relative importance just by staring and thinking. The problem with designing in a vacuum, trying to have every piece designed before any code is written, is that the designer(s) can end up spending lots of effort on parts of the design that turn out to be unimportant.

The use of data abstraction helps make the iterations less painful, by reducing the likelihood that a particular change will involve going all the way back to square one. Even if the change is a major one, if the original classes were well designed, and implementation dependencies hidden, it is often feasible to fix the design in C++. A C project faced with a change of the same magnitude would have had to start over or (due to time pressures) press on with the original design and hope for the best.

11.3.3   The experts build the classes, everyone uses them

Building C++ classes is harder than using them; the fundamental classes on a project should be designed and built by the most skilled and experienced staff. Data abstraction does not make issues such as storage management, bookkeeping, and implementation design go away. The benefit is that only the class designer worries about these issues; the users do not. The class designer must still get them right for the project to be a success. The benefits come from the fact that once the fundamental classes are right, the rest of the project members can use them without getting another chance to mess up the bookkeeping.

11.3.4   Don't use everything all at once

C++ has a lot of features; not all are appropriate for every application. Some new C++ programmers try to use every new feature "because it's there." While some experimentation is an important part of the learning process, it is important to remember the difference between an experiment and a product. It is easy to get carried away with new toys, which can lead to baroque designs. Multiple inheritance, implicit type conversions, and operator overloading are especially prone to this. Each programmer should be able to explain why the use of a particular feature will make the code faster, safer, or easier to understand.

11.3.5   Use general purpose libraries

One of the biggest benefits of C++ is that it allows the programmer to operate at a higher level of abstraction. When a library of container class templates is used, the fundamental building blocks used in the detailed design process are no longer arrays, structs, and pointers; they become lists, sets, bags, maps, and blocks. This frees the implementors from the drudgery (and bugs) involved with reimplementing those data structures from scratch every time. Coding goes significantly faster when libraries are used aggressively; a programmer can just use a `List<String>` without having to worry about implementing the `List` or `String` data structures.

11.3.6   Allocate more compiler cycles

C++ allows a programmer to program at a higher level than in C, especially if libraries are used. However, even though the programmers do not have to worry about the low-level details, the compiler and linker still do. A single line of code does more, so it takes more computer cycles to compile. This is especially true when templates are used.

Computer cycles are getting cheaper relative to human cycles, so this is a good tradeoff; but do not forget that you are making a tradeoff, and that increased automation requires increased computer cycles.

11.3.7 Expect larger object code sizes

The amount of object code generated for each line of C++ source may be surprisingly large. This is not a language problem—adding two integers generates the same code in C++ as it does in C. Rather, it is a consequence of the fact that a single line of code can do more in C++. Aggressive use of inline expansion can make this effect even stronger.

C++ makes libraries easier to use; but libraries also cause larger object sizes. You can expect a library that is general purpose to be larger than hand crafted code that implements only those functions required for a particular application. Separating the library into different object files can help reduce this effect, but in practice it does not eliminate it.

11.3.8 Converting existing C code to C++

In general, you should not bother, especially if the C code is not under active development. C++ and C are link compatible, and programmers seem to be able to simultaneously maintain code written in both languages. (Very few language constructs compile in both languages but do different things.) You will have to write C++ headers that declare the C functions, but unless the C source code is broken, don't fix it. The makefiles can remember which compiler to use for each file.

11.4 Developing an asset base

General purpose libraries are widely available; but you may be unable to purchase libraries that encapsulate the important concepts of your application domain. Organizations that are developing a suite of products that operate in the same application domain may find it worthwhile to develop their own libraries of reusable assets. When done right, this can be very cost effective; but projects often underestimate the cost of building a reusable class library.

Reuse cannot be a hobby. Do not expect to build reusable classes by asking your developers to produce them as a side effect of building an application. Building a reusable class is several times more expensive than building a class that is just good enough for the application at hand; the reusable class must be more general, more robust, more extensively tested, more extensively documented, and more extensively supported. These extra activities must be explicitly funded for them to take place.

Organizing the development of an asset base as an explicit activity also helps make sure that different libraries will behave in a consistent manner; if half of your libraries use one way to iterate through a collection and half use another, it will be a source of confusion to the users.

11.5   A closing thought

C++ does not remove the need for designers and programmers with experience, taste, and judgment. Rather, it gives such designers and programmers tools to help them apply their skills at a higher conceptual level. Bad programmers will still write bad programs in C++; but good ones can use the features of C++ to quickly build programs that are fast, easy to understand, and easy to maintain.

11.6   In short

- Schedules must allow for the learning curve.

- C++ is an excellent general purpose language, but a more specialized language may be appropriate for applications that fit its niche.

- Adopt C++ gradually, starting by using it as a better C, progressing to data abstraction, and then to object-oriented programming.

- C++ front loads the design process.

- Don't use everything at once.

- Expect iteration on your designs.

- It is easier to use classes than to build them.

- Use general purpose libraries.

- Higher level languages require more computer cycles.

- Expect your programs to have larger object sizes.

- Do not convert existing C to C++ unless you are planning on doing significant new development on it.

- Reuse cannot be a hobby.

11.7 Questions

1. How does the size of the project affect the decision to use C++? How does it impact whether it makes more sense to move right to object-oriented programming or to move in gradually?

2. How might a project with severe constraints on the object size move to C++? What processes might you put in place to track the object size?

3. Doesn't having the most experienced programmers build the class create a programming "elite"? Isn't this disruptive? How do programmers who are not part of the elite learn to write classes?

4. How would you track the iteration on the design to make sure that real progress was being made?

Index